D1649590

ENGLISH
FOLK SONGS

Edited by
Ralph Vaughan
Williams
and
A. L. Lloyd

English 🐧 *Journeys*

PENGUIN BOOKS

Published by the Penguin Group
Penguin Books Ltd, 80 Strand, London WC2R ORL, England
Penguin Group (USA) Inc., 375 Hudson Street, New York, New York 10014, USA
Penguin Group (Canada), 90 Eglinton Avenue East, Suite 700, Toronto, Ontario, Canada M4P 2Y3
(a division of Pearson Penguin Canada Inc.)
Penguin Ireland, 25 St Stephen's Green, Dublin 2, Ireland (a division of Penguin Books Ltd)
Penguin Group (Australia), 250 Camberwell Road, Camberwell, Victoria 3124, Australia
(a division of Pearson Australia Group Pty Ltd)
Penguin Books India Pvt Ltd, 11 Community Centre, Panchsheel Park, New Delhi – 110 017, India
Penguin Group (NZ), 67 Apollo Drive, Rosedale, Auckland 0632, New Zealand
(a division of Pearson New Zealand Ltd)
Penguin Books (South Africa) (Pty) Ltd, 24 Sturdee Avenue,
Rosebank, Johannesburg 2196, South Africa

Penguin Books Ltd, Registered Offices: 80 Strand, London WC2R ORL, England

www.penguin.com

First published as *The Penguin Book of English Folk Songs* 1959
Published under the current title in Penguin Books 2009
This special edition for Sandpiper Books / Postscript published 2011

5

Copyright © A. L. Lloyd and the representatives of R. Vaughan Williams, 1959
All rights reserved

The moral right of the authors has been asserted

Set in Monotype Garamond
Typeset by Rowland Phototypesetting Ltd, Bury St Edmunds, Suffolk
Printed in England by Clays Ltd, St Ives plc

Except in the United States of America, this book is sold subject
to the condition that it shall not, by way of trade or otherwise, be lent,
re-sold, hired out, or otherwise circulated without the publisher's
prior consent in any form of binding or cover other than that in
which it is published and without a similar condition including this
condition being imposed on the subsequent purchaser

ISBN: 978-0-141-19092-1

www.greenpenguin.co.uk

MIX
Paper from
responsible sources
FSC® C018179
www.fsc.org

Penguin Books is committed to a sustainable
future for our business, our readers and our
planet. This book is made from paper certified
by the Forest Stewardship Council.

Contents

Introduction

An old Suffolk labourer with a fine folk song repertory and a delicate, rather gnat-like voice, once remarked: 'I used to be reckoned a good singer before these here *tunes* came in.' The *tunes* he spoke of with such scorn had come in with a vengeance, and it seemed that his kind of songs, once so admired, would be lost under the flood of commercial popular music. However, folk songs are tough, and show an obstinate will to survive. Of recent years, they have begun to reassert themselves in places where formerly only *tunes* were heard, and now it seems that many young people, whose musical nourishment had been limited to whatever came to them in canned form from the Charing Cross Road, are looking to folk music for something that they can take and re-make as their own. The ceilidh, the folk-singing party, is becoming a part of urban social life, and the voice of the revival folk-singer makes itself heard in youth hostels, city pubs, skiffle cellars, even in jazz clubs. It is a curious but welcome phenomenon, this revival of folk music as a city music. It seems that many taking part in that revival have come to appreciate British balladry through their interest in jazz. A search for the roots of jazz leads to American folk song, and a search for the origins of American folk song leads the astonished enthusiast back home to his own traditional music. It is to the partisans of the new folk song revival that this book is first addressed, but we hope, too, that our selection will contain some delightful surprises for those who have been singing folk songs for years.

The songs we have chosen are all taken from the *Journal of the Folk Song Society* and its continuation, the *Journal of the English Folk Dance and Song Society*. The Folk Song Society was founded in 1898, as the culmination of the work of Baring Gould, Lucy Broadwood, Fuller Maitland, Frank Kidson, and others in rescuing the beautiful traditional music of England from oblivion. The Folk Song Society and its successor, the English Folk Dance and Song Society, have published annually, as their *Journal*, a small volume of the songs discovered by their members. Many of the songs have found their way to a wide public, being printed in settings for voice and piano, for choir, or in other forms. We have included none of these in the present volume, but have confined ourselves to songs and variants unpublished outside the pages of the *Journals*. Thus, this book consists of versions of songs that have hitherto remained in what is practically a private collection. We have found our choice hard to make, for in this book we have room for only a small portion of the two thousand or so British traditional melodies contained in the *Journals*. Reluctantly, we decided to leave out all occupational and seasonal songs, such as Christmas carols, harvest songs, and sailors' shanties. These may be included in a future volume.

This is a book to sing from. To make the songs singable, the editorial hand has been used where necessary.

We assure our readers that the melodies have not been doctored, but are as the collector took them from the traditional singer. With the words, the case is rather different. Music is a matter of emotion, words of logic. If a bad singer mars a tune, we either keep it as it is, or leave it out; in no case do we alter it. However, if a forgetful singer omits verses or lines, or knows the song only in imperfect form, we do not hesitate, in compiling a book for popular use, to complete the song from other traditional sources. Phillips Barry, a responsible American folk song scholar, speaks for us: 'Different obligations bind the maker of a scientific work to be thrown to the lions of scholarship and the maker of a practical work for people who like singing.... The editor of a practical work has the right and is under the duty to make both singable and understandable the song he edits.... Both singer and scholar, nevertheless, into whose hands the book may fall, have today a right ... to know both the extent and the sources of editorial changes and restorations.'

Accordingly, in several instances we have collated various versions of song-texts, whether recorded from oral sources or printed on broadsides. Where we have done this, we say so in our Notes, and we give the source of our borrowing. In very rare cases, and only where it seemed otherwise very hard to make the text fit the tune, we have ventured to cancel a few words, or to add interjections such as 'oh' or 'and', in order to complete the scansion of a line. In most cases, irregular lines have been left irregular, for therein lies some of the beauty of folk song; any folk singer worth his salt delights in variation, and some of the happiest rhythmical effects may come from making the tune fit the words instead of adapting the text to the tune.

In a few cases, we have shortened songs that seemed overlong for what they had to say. On the other hand, we have not hesitated to include words, verses, or whole texts which earlier collectors prudishly modified or omitted as being objectionable. The old habit of cleaning-up or even entirely rewriting the texts led to the false supposition that folk songs are always 'quite nice'. The folk singer has no objection to plain speech. He is likely to be forthright in his treatment of the pleasures and pains of love, though he may class some songs as 'outway rude' which we think quite harmless. In restoring song-texts that had hitherto been published only in bowdlerized form, we have referred to the collectors' original manuscripts.

We have said that the melodies represent the songs as the collectors reported them. The remark needs some qualification. In a few cases the *Journal* versions showed errors of musical grammar, and these have been corrected. One or two tunes needed re-barring. Several of the melodies have been transposed, in the interests of orderliness and singability. Otherwise, we have been at pains to preserve the collectors' impression of what their informants were actually singing. It must be confessed that when, perhaps under the influence of modern convention, a singer has weakened certain phrases of a fine modal tune, the temptation to 'correct' his singing is great. We have resisted that temptation. In one instance, however, it may be considered that we have cheated slightly. The singer of No. 29, *The Grey Cock*, constantly sang a final F on the recording. Her son remembers that she used to sing a final D. The D preserves the modal character of this beautiful tune, whereas the F comes as a disappointment. In our transcription we have retained the D, but have indicated the F as a variant.

We would like to give a few suggestions for singing the songs in this book. The ideal way to sing an English folk song, of course, is unaccompanied. Our melodies were made to be sung that way, and much of their tonal beauty and delightful suppleness comes from the fact that they have been traditionally free from harmonic or rhythmic accompaniment. They are best suited to stand on their own, and we rather agree with the Dorset countryman who commented on a professional singer of folk songs: 'Of course, it's nice for him to have the piano when he's singing, but it does make it very awkward for the listener.'

However, for those to whom the unaccompanied voice seems naked, there is no harm in adding a few supporting chords on the pianoforte, guitar, or other instrument, provided the chords are in keeping with the style of the tune. Special care needs to be taken when accompanying modal tunes, where the chords should be strictly in the mode. As to which instruments should or should not be used for folk song accompaniment, this is entirely a matter of choice. The fashionable guitar has no more traditional sanction than the less fashionable pianoforte. The concertina, mouth-organ, fiddle, banjo, zither, spoons, bones, even the harmonium have all been used as accompaniment to country singers without necessarily resulting in a performance that sounds more 'right' than that given by the voice un-adorned. On pages 9 and 10 we print a few examples of the way in which, in our opinion, the songs might be harmonized. But we hope that our readers will sing the songs unaccompanied as much as possible.

It should not be necessary to impress on our readers that this volume does not offer them what is mere clownish nonsense or only of antiquarian interest. Béla Bartók, who knew more about folk music than any other musician of our time, once said: 'Folk melodies are a real model of the highest artistic perfection. To my mind, on a small scale, they are masterpieces just as much as, in the world of larger forms, a fugue by Bach or a Mozart sonata.' We believe that the songs in this book are not only full of classical beauty, but are the foundations on which all more matured musical art must be built. This has been recognized in every country except England; and even here we are beginning to realize that, in the words of Virginia Woolf (a writer who knew nothing about folk music, but whose words are extraordinarily applicable to our case): 'Masterpieces are not single and solitary births, they are the outcome of many years of thinking in common, of thinking by the body of the people, so that the experience of the mass is behind the single voice.'

So, in singing these songs, you may not only have great enjoyment, but you may be showing to some mute inglorious Milton the way which will lead him to musical self-expression. Sincerely, we wish you joy.

R. V. W. AND A. L. L.

A Note on the Presentation of the Tunes

This modest selection of folk songs was almost ready for the press when Dr Vaughan Williams died. A few problems remained to be solved concerning the presentation of the tunes. For the way these have been dealt with in the absence of the wise and experienced partner, the responsibility must be mine.

In continental folk song collections, where the songs are presented un-set, and only the melody-line is given, it has become customary to transpose all the tunes to a common finalis, usually G. By that means, melodies may be easier compared and analysed by those wishing to do so. Owing to the range of some of our tunes Dr Vaughan Williams and I had not found the final G always convenient. Moreover, since these songs are intended to be sung rather than merely looked at, we had not considered ourselves bound to the custom of the common finalis. However, looking over the tunes as we had prepared them, I found that the majority had, as it happened, been transcribed to end either on G or D. It seemed only common sense to bring the few remaining melodies into line. Thus, in this selection, about half the melodies end on G, the other half on D, according to their range and modal character.

It is well known that the scales on which many of our folk tunes are based are not the same as the major and minor with which we are most familiar. Some of these scales belong to the family of what are loosely called 'Greek' modes, some are considered as gapped scales because certain steps are consistently missing, while a few show peculiar structures which the scholars have hardly begun to classify as yet. None of this need frighten the reader who has no mind for musical technicalities. Certainly it never worried the traditional singer, who could not read music – perhaps could not read at all – but could sing spontaneously in what the theorists explain as the Dorian or Mixolydian mode.*

Our folk song editors have found it hard to throw off the habit of hearing every tune under the influence of the conventional major-minor system, and it has been usual to give 'standard' key signatures to folk tunes, even though that might involve constantly cancelling the signature by putting a natural sign before certain tones every time they appear. Some feel this practice to be illogical (it has been compared to putting up a *No Smoking* sign in a place where tobacco is unknown). On the other hand, some will argue that the hasty eye might well misread a modal tune unless given full warning where the 'odd' notes occur.

How were we to present our tunes? In the familiar way, with a major or minor signature? Or in the newer fashion, in which one refrains from putting into the key signature sharps or flats that do not occur in the

---

* The fact seems to have surprised some pioneers of the folk song movement. Dr Vaughan Williams had a story of one scholar who, confronted with some notations newly taken down from a folk singer, declared: 'These must be wrong. Nobody's going to tell me that an uneducated villager sings correctly in the Dorian mode when, as often as not, even our trained musicians don't know what the Dorian is!'

tune? For better or for worse, I have decided to adopt the latter style. Thereby, perhaps, those without formal musical education may find the songs easier to read, while those with some knowledge of musical theory may reach a better understanding of the tunes.

A. L. L.

SPECIMEN ACCOMPANIMENTS
BY R. VAUGHAN WILLIAMS

SALISBURY PLAIN

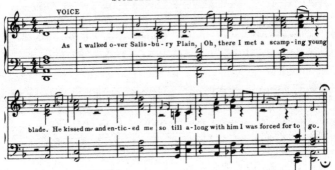

BANKS OF GREEN WILLOW

sail right o'er the o - cean A - long with young John - ny.

THE BASKET OF EGGS

VOICE

Down in Sand-bank fields, two sail-ors they were walking, Their pockets were both

lined with gold, And as to-geth-er they were talk-ing, A fair maid there they

did be-hold, With a lit-tle bas-ket stand-ing by her As she sat down to

take her ease. To car-ry it for her one of them of-fered. The

an-swer was: 'Sir if you please.'

ALL THINGS ARE QUITE SILENT

Sung by Ted Baines, Lower Beeding, Sussex (R.V.W. 1904)

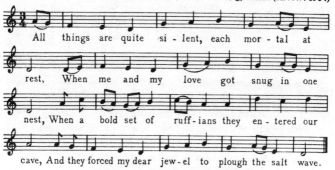

All things are quite silent, each mortal at rest,
When me and my love got snug in one nest,
When a bold set of ruffians they entered our cave,
And they forced my dear jewel to plough the salt wave.

I begged hard for my sailor as though I begged for life.
They'd not listen to me although a fond wife.
Saying: 'The king he wants sailors, to the sea he must go,'
And they've left me lamenting in sorrow and woe.

Through green fields and meadow we ofttimes did walk,
And sweet conversation of love we have talked,
With the birds in the woodland so sweetly did sing,
And the lovely thrushes' voices made the valleys to ring.

Although my love's gone I will not be cast down.
Who knows but my sailor may once more return?
And will make me amends for all trouble and strife,
And my true love and I might live happy for life.

Ralph Vaughan Williams and A. L. Lloyd

AS SYLVIE WAS WALKING

Sung by Mrs Aston, Moonee Ponds, Vic., Australia (T.A. 1911)

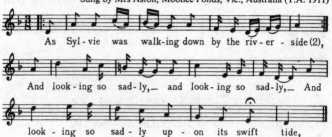

As Syl-vie was walk-ing down by the riv-er - side (2),
And look-ing so sad-ly,— and look-ing so sad-ly,— And
look - ing so sad - ly up - on its swift tide,

As Sylvie was walking down by the riverside,
As Sylvie was walking down by the riverside,
And looking so sadly, and looking so sadly,
And looking so sadly upon its swift tide,

She thought on the lover that left her in pride,
She thought on the lover that left her in pride,
On the banks of the meadow, on the banks of the meadow
On the banks of the meadow she sat down and cried.

And as she sat weeping, a young man came by,
And as she sat weeping, a young man came by.
'What ails you, my jewel, what ails you, my jewel,
What ails you, my jewel and makes you to cry?'

'I once had a sweetheart and now I have none.
I once had a sweetheart and now I have none.
He's a-gone and he's leaved me, he's a-gone, he's deceived me,
He's a-gone and he's leaved me in sorrow to mourn.

'One night in sweet slumber, I dream that I see,
One night in sweet slumber, I dream that I see,
My own dearest true love, my own dearest true love,
My own dearest true love come smiling to me.

'But when I awoke and I found it not so,
But when I awoke and I found it not so,
Mine eyes were like fountains, mine eyes were like fountains,
Mine eyes were like fountains where the water doth flow.

'I'll spread sail of silver and I'll steer towards the sun,
I'll spread sail of silver and I'll steer towards the sun,
And my false love will weep, and my false love will weep,
And my false love will weep for me after I'm gone.'

THE BANKS OF GREEN WILLOW

Sung by Mrs Overd, Langport, Somerset (C.J.S. 1904)

Go and get your father's good will,
And get your mother's money,
And sail right o'er the ocean
Along with young Johnny.

She had not been a-sailing
Been sailing many days, O,
Before she want some woman's help
And could not get any.

Oh, fetch me a silk napkin
To tie her head up easy,
And I'll throw her overboard
Both she and her baby.

Oh, they fetched him a napkin
And bound her head so easy,
And overboard he threw his love,
Both she and her baby.

See how my love do tumble,
See how my love do taver,
See how my love do try to swim,
That makes my heart quaver.

Oh, make my love a coffin
Of the gold that shines yellow,
And she shall be buried
By the banks of green willow.

Ralph Vaughan Williams and A. L. Lloyd

THE BANKS OF NEWFOUNDLAND

Sung by John Farr, Gwithian, Cornwall (J.E.T. 1926)

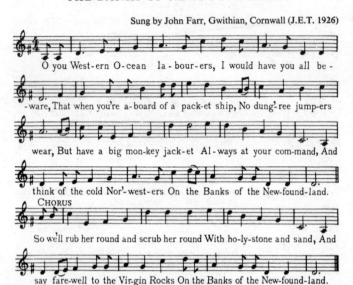

O you Western Ocean labourers, I would have you all beware, That when you're aboard of a packet ship, No dungaree jumpers wear, But have a big monkey jacket Always at your command, And think of the cold Nor'-westers On the Banks of the New-found-land.

CHORUS

So we'll rub her round and scrub her round With holy-stone and sand, And say fare-well to the Virgin Rocks On the Banks of the New-found-land.

O you Western Ocean labourers,
I would have you all beware,
That when you're aboard of a packet-ship,
No dungaree jumpers wear,
But have a big monkey jacket
Always at your command,
And think of the cold Nor'westers
On the Banks of the Newfoundland.

Chorus: So we'll rub her round and scrub her round
With holystone and sand,
And say farewell to the Virgin Rocks
On the Banks of the Newfoundland.

As I lay in my bunk one night
A-dreaming all alone,
I dreamt I was in Liverpool,
'Way up in Marylebone,
With my true love beside of me,
And a jug of ale in hand,
When I woke quite broken-hearted
On the Banks of Newfoundland.

We had one Lynch from Ballinahinch,
Jimmy Murphy and Mike Moore;
It was in the winter of sixty-two,
Those sea-boys suffered sore,
For they'd pawned their clothes in Liver-
And sold them out of hand,   [pool,
Not thinking of the cold Nor'westers
On the Banks of Newfoundland.

14

We had one female passenger,
Bridget Riley was her name,
To her I promised marriage
And on me she had a claim.
She tore up her flannel petticoats
To make mittens for our hands,
For she couldn't see the sea-boys freeze
On the Banks of Newfoundland.

And now we're off Sandy Hook, my boys,
And the land's all covered with snow.
The tug-boat will take our hawser
And for New York we will tow;
And when we arrive at the Black Ball dock,
The boys and girls there will stand,
We'll bid adieu to the packet-ships
And the Banks of Newfoundland.

THE BANKS OF SWEET PRIMROSES

Sung by Mrs Vaisey, Hampshire (L.E.B. 1892)

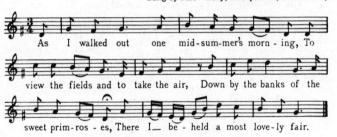

As I walked out one mid-sum-mer's morn-ing, To view the fields and to take the air, Down by the banks of the sweet prim-ros-es, There I be-held a most love-ly fair.

As I walked out one midsummer's morning,
To view the fields and to take the air,
Down by the banks of the sweet primroses,
There I beheld a most lovely fair.

I said: 'Fair maid, where can you be a-going,
And what's the occasion of all your grief?
I'll make you as happy as any lady,
If you will grant me one small relief.'

'Stand off, stand off, thou false deceiver!
You're a false deceitful man, 'tis plain.
'Tis you that is causing my poor heart to wander,
And to give me comfort is all in vain.

'Now I'll go down to some lonesome valley,
Where no man on earth there shall me find,
Where the pretty small birds do change their voices,
And every moment blows blusterous wind.'

THE BASKET OF EGGS

Sung by H. Burstow, Horsham, Sussex (R.V.W. 1903)

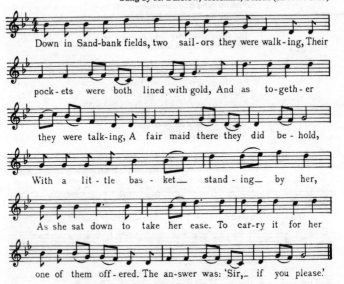

Down in Sand-bank fields, two sail-ors they were walk-ing, Their
pock-ets were both lined with gold, And as to-geth-er
they were talk-ing, A fair maid there they did be-hold,
With a lit-tle bas-ket__ stand-ing__ by her,
As she sat down to take her ease. To car-ry it for her
one of them off-ered. The an-swer was: 'Sir,__ if you please.'

Down in Sandbank fields, two sailors they were walking,
Their pockets were both lined with gold,
And as together they were talking,
A fair maid there they did behold,
With a little basket standing by her,
As she sat down to take her ease.
To carry it for her one of them offered.
The answer was: 'Sir, if you please.'

One of these sailors took the basket.
'There's eggs in the basket, please take care;
And if by chance you should out-walk me,
At the Half-way House please leave them there.'
Behold these sailors, they did outwalk her,
The Half-way House they did pass by.
This pretty damsel she laughed at their fancy,
And on the sailors she kept her eye.

When these two sailors came unto an ale-house,
There they did call for a pint of wine,
Saying: 'Landlord, landlord, what fools in this nation!
This young maid from her eggs we've twined.
O landlord, landlord, bring us some bacon.
We have got these eggs and we'll have some dressed.'
Behold, these sailors were much mistaken,
As you shall say when you hear the rest.

'Twas then the landlord he went to the basket,
Expecting of some eggs to find.
He said: 'Young man, you're much mistaken,
Instead of eggs I've found a child.'
Then one of them sat down to weeping.
The other said: 'It's not worth while.
Here's fifty guineas I'll give to the baby,
If any woman will take the child.'

This pretty young damsel she sat by the fire,
And she had a shawl drawn over her face.
She said: 'I'll take it and kindly use it,
When first I see the money paid.'
One of the sailors threw down the money.
Great favour to the babe was shown.
'Since it is so, then let's be friendly,
For you know, this child is yours and mine.

'Don't you remember a-dancing with Nancy,
As long ago as last Easter day?'
'Oh yes, and I do, and she pleased my fancy,
So now the fiddler I have paid.'
One of the sailors went up to the basket,
And he kicked the basket over and o'er.
'Since it is so, may we all be contented,
But I'm hanged if I'll like eggs any more.'

Ralph Vaughan Williams and A. L. Lloyd

BENJAMIN BOWMANEER

Sung by Sarah Foster, Sedbergh (M.E.S. n.d.)

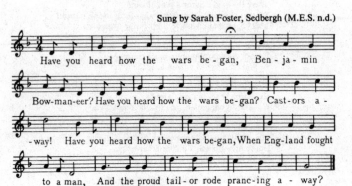

Have you heard how the wars be-gan, Ben-ja-min Bow-man-eer? Have you heard how the wars be-gan? Cast-ors a-way! Have you heard how the wars be-gan, When Eng-land fought to a man, And the proud tail-or rode pranc-ing a-way?

Have you heard how the wars began,
Benjamin Bowmaneer?
Have you heard how the wars began?
Castors away!
Have you heard how the wars began,
When England fought to a man,
And the proud tailor rode prancing away?

Of his shear board he made a horse,
Benjamin Bowmaneer.
Of his shear board he made a horse.
Castors away!
Of his shear board he made a horse,
All for him to ride across.
So the proud tailor rode prancing away.

Of his scissors he made bridle bits,
Benjamin Bowmaneer.
Of his scissors he made bridle bits.
Castors away!
Of his scissors he made bridle bits,
To keep the horse in its wits.
So the proud tailor rode prancing away.

As the tailor rode o'er the lea,
Benjamin Bowmaneer,
As the tailor rode o'er the lea,
Castors away!
As the tailor rode o'er the lea,
He spied a flea all on his knee.
So the proud tailor rode prancing away.

18

Of his needle he made a spear,
Benjamin Bowmaneer.
Of his needle he made a spear,
Castors away!
Of his needle he made a spear,
To prick that flea through its ear.
So the proud tailor rode prancing away.

Of his thimble he made a bell,
Benjamin Bowmaneer.
Of his thimble he made a bell.
Castors away!
Of his thimble he made a bell,
To ring the flea's funeral knell.
So the proud tailor rode prancing away.

'Twas thus that the wars began,
 Benjamin Bowmaneer.
'Twas thus that the wars began.
 Castors away!
'Twas thus that the wars began,
 When England fought to a man.
 And the proud tailor rode prancing away.

THE BLACKSMITH

Sung by Mrs Powell, nr Weobley, Herefordshire (R.V.W. 1909)

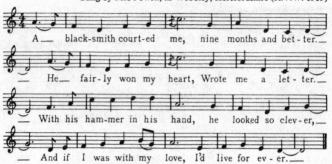

A blacksmith courted me, nine months and better.
He fairly won my heart, wrote me a letter.
With his hammer in his hand, he looked so clever,
And if I was with my love, I'd live for ever.

And where is my love gone, with his cheek like roses,
And his good black billycock on, decked with primroses?
I'm afraid the scorching sun will shine and burn his beauty,
And if I was with my love, I'd do my duty.

Strange news is come to town, strange news is carried,
Strange news flies up and down that my love is married.
I wish them both much joy, though they don't hear me,
And may God reward him well for slighting of me.

'What did you promise when you sat beside me?
You said you would marry me, and not deny me.'
'If I said I'd marry you, it was only for to try you,
So bring your witness, love, and I'll never deny you.'

'Oh, witness have I none save God Almighty.
And He'll reward you well for slighting of me.'
Her lips grew pale and white, it made her poor heart tremble
To think she loved one, and he proved deceitful.

THE BOLD BENJAMIN

Sung by Mr Taunton, Corscombe, Dorset (H.E.D.H. 1907)

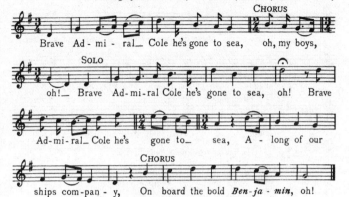

Brave Admiral Cole he's gone to sea, oh, my boys, oh! Brave Admiral Cole he's gone to sea, oh! Brave Admiral Cole he's gone to sea, A - long of our ships com-pan - y, On board the bold *Ben-ja-min*, oh!

Brave Admiral Cole he's gone to sea, oh, my boys, oh!
Brave Admiral Cole he's gone to sea, oh!
Brave Admiral Cole he's gone to sea,
Along of our ship's company,
On board the bold *Benjamin*, oh!

We sailed our course away for Spain, oh, my boys, oh!
We sailed our course away for Spain, oh!
We sailed our course away for Spain,
Our silver and gold for to gain,
On board the bold *Benjamin*, oh!

We sailed out five hundred men, oh, my boys, oh!
We sailed out five hundred men, oh!
We sailed out five hundred men,
And brought back but sixty one.
They were lost in bold *Benjamin*, oh!

And when we came to Blackwall, oh, my boys, oh!
And when we came to Blackwall, oh!
And when we came to Blackwall,
Our captain so loudly did call:
'Here comes the bold *Benjamin*, oh!'

Here's the mothers crying for their sons, oh, my boys, oh!
Here's the mothers crying for their sons, oh!
Here's the mothers crying for their sons,
And the widows for their husbands
That were lost in bold *Benjamin*, oh!

THE BRAMBLE BRIAR

Sung by Mrs Joiner, Chiswell Green, Herts. (L.E.B. 1914)

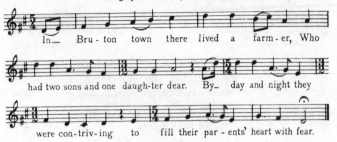

In Bruton town there lived a farmer,
Who had two sons and one daughter dear.
By day and night they were contriving
To fill their parents' heart with fear.

He told his secrets to no other,
But unto her brother this he said:
'I think our servant courts our sister.
I think they has a great mind to wed.
I'll put an end to all their courtship.
I'll send him silent to his grave.'

They asked him to go a-hunting,
Without any fear or strife,
And these two bold and wicked villains
They took away this young man's life.

And in the ditch there was no water,
Where only bush and'briars grew.
They could not hide the blood of slaughter,
So in the ditch his body they threw.

When they returned home from hunting,
She asked for her servant-man.
'I ask because I see you whisper,
So brothers tell me if you can.'

'O sister, sister, you do offend me,
Because you so examine me.
We've lost him where we've been a-hunting,
No more of him we could not see.'

As she lay dreaming on her pillow,
She thought she saw her heart's delight;
By her bed side as she lay weeping,
He was dressed all in his bloody coat.

22

Don't weep for me, my dearest jewel,
Don't weep for me nor care nor pine,
For your two brothers killed me so cruel –
In such a place you may me find.'

As she rose early the very next morning,
With heavy sigh and bitter groan,
The only love that she admired,
She found in the ditch where he was thrown.

The blood upon his lips was drying.
Her tears were salt as any brine.
She sometimes kissed him, sometimes crying:
'Here lies the dearest friend of mine.'

Three days and nights she did sit by him,
And her poor heart was filled with woe,
Till cruel hunger crept upon her,
And home she was obliged to go.

When she returned to her brothers:
' Sister, what makes you look so thin?'
Brother, don't you ask the reason,
' And for his sake you shall be hung!'

THE BROOMFIELD HILL

Sung by Mrs Powell, Weobley, Herefordshire (E.M.L. & R.V.W. 1910)

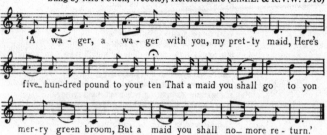

'A wager, a wager with you, my pretty maid, Here's five hundred pound to your ten That a maid you shall go to yon merry green broom, But a maid you shall no more return.'

'A wager, a wager with you, my pretty
  maid,
Here's five hundred pound to your ten
That a maid you shall go to yon merry
  green broom,
But a maid you shall no more return.'

'A wager, a wager with you, kind sir,
With your hundred pounds to my ten,
That a maid I will go to yon merry
  green broom,
And a maid I will boldly return.'

Now when that she came to this merry
  green broom,
Found her true love was fast in a sleep,
With a fine finished rose, and a new suit
  of clothes,
And a bunch of green broom at his feet.

Then three times she went from the
  crown of his head,
And three times from the sole of his feet,
And three times she kissed his red rosy
  cheeks
As he lay fast in a sleep.

Then she took a gold ring from off her
  hand,
And put that on his right thumb,
And that was to let her true love to
  know
That she had been there and was gone.

As soon as he had awoke from his sleep,
Found his true love had been there and
  gone,
It was then he remembered upon the
  cost,
When he thought of the wager he'd lost.

Three times he called for his horse and
  his man,
The horse he'd once bought so dear,
Saying: 'Why didn't you wake me out
  of my sleep,
When my lady, my true love, was here?'

'Three times did I call to you, master,
And three times did I blow with my
  horn,
But out of your sleep I could not awake
Till your lady, your true love, was gone.'

'Had I been awake when my true love was here,
  Of her I would had my will;
If not, the pretty birds in this merry green broom
  With her blood they should all had their fill.'

THE COCK-FIGHT (THE BONNY GREY)

Sung by J. Collinson, Casterton, Lancashire (C.J.S. 1905)

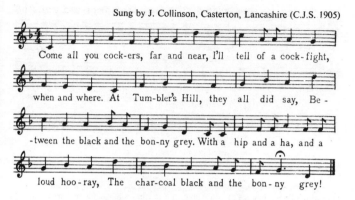

Come all you cock-ers, far and near, I'll tell of a cock-fight, when and where. At Tum-bler's Hill, they all did say, Be-tween the black and the bon-ny grey. With a hip and a ha, and a loud hoo-ray, The char-coal black and the bon-ny grey!

Come all you cockers, far and near,
I'll tell of a cock-fight, when and where.
At Tumbler's Hill, they all did say,
Between the black and the bonny grey.
    With a hip and a ha, and a loud hooray,
    The charcoal black and the bonny grey!

It's to the house to take a sup;
The cock-fight it was soon made up.
Ten guineas a side these cocks will play,
The charcoal black and the bonny grey.

Lord Derby he came swaggering down.
'I'll lay ten guineas to half a crown,
If the charcoal black he gets fair play,
He'll rip the wings off the bonny grey.'

These cocks hadn't struck past two or three blows,
When the Biggar lads cried: 'Now you'll lose.'
Which made us all both wan and pale.
We wished we'd fought for a gallon of ale.

And the cocks they at it, one, two, three,
And the charcoal black got struck in the eye,
They picked him up to see fair play,
But the black wouldn't fight with the bonny grey.

With the silver breast and the silver wing,
Six brothers of his fought before the king.
With a hip and a ha, and a loud hooray,
And away we went with our bonny grey!

THE CRUEL MOTHER

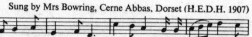

Sung by Mrs Bowring, Cerne Abbas, Dorset (H.E.D.H. 1907)

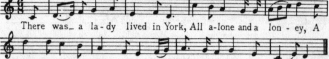

There was a lady lived in York,
All alone and a loney,
A farmer's son he courted her
All down by the greenwood sidey.

He courted her for seven long years.
At last she proved in child by him.

She pitched her knee against a tree,
And there she found great misery.

She pitched her back against a thorn,
And there she had her baby born.

She drew the fillet off her head.
She bound the baby's hands and legs.

She drew a knife both long and sharp.
She pierced the baby's innocent heart.

She wiped the knife upon the grass.
The more she wiped, the blood run fast.

She washed her hands all in the spring,
Thinking to turn a maid again.

As she was going to her father's hall,
She saw three babes a-playing at ball.

One dressed in silk, the other in satin,
The other star-naked as ever was born.

O, dear baby, if you was mine,
I'd dress you in silk and satin so fine.

O, dear mother, I once was thine.
You never would dress me coarse or fine.

The coldest earth it was my bed.
The green grass was my coverlet.

O, mother, mother, for your sin,
Heaven gate you shall not enter in.

There is a fire beyond hell's gate,
And there you'll burn both early and late.

THE DAUGHTER OF PEGGY, O

Sung by Charles Spiller, Pitminster, Som. (C.J.S. 1908)

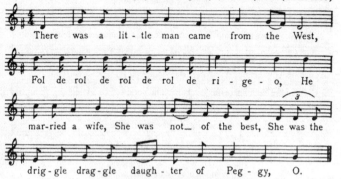

There was a little man came from the West,
Fol de rol de rol de rol de rigeo, He married a wife, She was not— of the best, She was the driggle draggle daughter of Peggy, O.

There was a little man came from the West,
    Fol de rol de rol de rol de rigeo,
He married a wife, she was not of the best,
    She was the driggle draggle daughter of Peggy, O.

She wouldn't card, she wouldn't spin,
She wouldn't work all in the kitchen.

When this good man came home from plough,
He says: 'My dear, is the dinner ready now?'

'Oh, if your dinner you must have,
Then get it yourself, I'm not your slave.'

'For I won't brew and I won't bake,
And I won't get my white hands black.'

This good man pulled his coat from his back,
And made his stick go widgy widgy whack.

'And if you won't do what I say now,
I'll take and yoke you to the plough.'

'Oh, I will card and I will spin,
And I will work all in the kitchen.'

'And I will bake and I will brew,
And I will cook your dinner for you.'

Ralph Vaughan Williams and A. L. Lloyd

DEATH AND THE LADY

Sung by Mr Baker, Maidstone, Kent (Anon. 1946)

As I walked out__ one morn in May, The birds did
sing and the lambs did play, The birds did sing and the
lambs did play, I met an old man, I met an old man,__
I met an old__ man by the way.

As I walked out one morn in May,
The birds did sing and the lambs did play,
The birds did sing and the lambs did play,
I met an old man, I met an old man,
I met an old man by the way.

His head was bald, his beard was grey,
His coat was of a myrtle shade,
I asked him what strange countryman,
Or what strange place, or what strange place,
Or what strange place he did belong.

'My name is Death, cannot you see?
Lords, dukes, and ladies bow down to me,
And you are one of those branches three,
And you fair maid, and you fair maid,
And you fair maid must come with me.'

'I'll give you gold and jewels rare,
I'll give you costly robes to wear,
I'll give you all my wealth in store,
If you'll let me live, if you'll let me live,
If you'll let me live a few years more.'

'Fair lady, lay your robes aside.
No longer glory in your pride.
And now, sweet maid, make no delay,
Your time is come, your time is come,
Your time is come and you must away.'

And not long after this fair maid died.
'Write on my tomb,' the lady cried,
'Here lies a poor distressed maid,
Whom Death now lately, whom Death now lately
Whom Death now lately hath betrayed.'

THE DEATH OF QUEEN JANE

Sung by Mrs Russell, Upwey, Dorset (H.E.D.H. 1907)

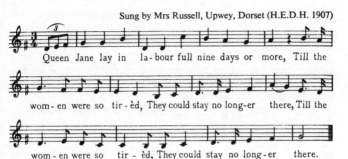

Queen Jane lay in la-bour full nine days or more, Till the wom-en were so tir-èd, They could stay no long-er there, Till the wom-en were so tir-èd, They could stay no long-er there.

Queen Jane lay in labour full nine days or more,
Till the women were so tirèd, they could stay no longer there. (2)

'Good women, good women, good women as ye be,
Do open my right side, and find my baby.'

'Oh no,' said the women. 'That never may be,
We will send for King Henry, and hear what he say.'

King Henry was sent for, King Henry did come:
'What do ail you, my lady, your eyes look so dim?'

'King Henry, King Henry, will you do one thing for me?
That's to open my right side, and find my baby.'

'Oh, no,' said King Henry. 'That's a thing I'll never do.
If I lose the flower of England, I shall lose the branch too.'

King Henry went mourning, and so did his men,
And so did the dear baby, for Queen Jane did die then.

And how deep was the mourning, how black were the bands,
How yellow, yellow were the flamboys they carried in their hands.

There was fiddling, aye, and dancing on the day the babe was born
But poor Queen Jane beloved lay cold as a stone.

Ralph Vaughan Williams and A. L. Lloyd

THE DESERTER FROM KENT

Sung by Mr Kemp, Elstead, Surrey (W.F. 1907)

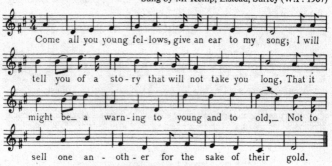

Come all you young fel-lows, give an ear to my song; I will
tell you of a sto-ry that will not take you long, That it
might be— a warn-ing to young and to old,— Not to
sell one an-oth-er for the sake of their gold.

Come all you young fellows, give an ear to my song;
I will tell you of a story that will not take you long,
That it might be a warning to young and to old,
Not to sell one another for the sake of their gold.

It happened about a twelvemonth ago,
There was two young fellows which most of us know,
Oh, one was a deserter as plain did appear,
Came from the west of Kent up to harvesting here.

Oh, what a deceiver he met with that year!
Both sat in an alehouse a-drinking of beer.
And all in good friendship he told what he knew,
Not thinking he'd been drinking all day with the foe.

Then after a while this man went away.
He met with two soldiers that very same day.
They were after a deserter, and to him did say,
Then he swore he'd been drinking with one all the day.

Then says the soldier: 'It'll answer our plan –
One guinea we'll give you; come show us the man.'
Then 'twas 'Come along with me' the fellow did say,
And down to the alehouse went William straightway.

Then in went the soldiers without dread or fear.
'What cheer?' says the fellow, then 'Give them some beer.
What regiment are you?' 'The Ninth,' they did say.
'What regiment are you? Come tell us, we pray.'

'No regiment at all,' so bold and so gay –
'Then we'll find one for you,' the soldiers did say.
They took him and kept him in hold all that night,
Until the next morning when it was day light.

Then to Maidstone Gaol they took him straightway,
Wrote down to his regiment: 'Come fetch him away.'
They marched him through town and they marched him through city,
With his hands tied behind him, and the ladies cried pity.

And now to conclude, I will tell you my hope:
May all such informers be faced with the rope.
They would sell one another for the sake of their gain,
And no doubt they will get just reward for their pain.

Ralph Vaughan Williams and A. L. Lloyd

THE DEVIL AND THE PLOUGHMAN

Sung by H. Burstow, Horsham, Sussex (R.V.W. 1903)

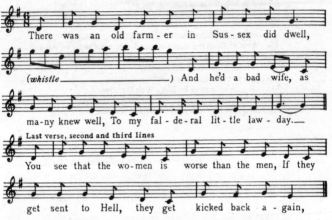

There was an old farmer in Sussex did dwell, *(whistle)*
And he'd a bad wife as many knew well,
To my fal-de-ral little law-day.

The Devil he came to the old man at plough, *(whistle)*
Saying: 'One of your family I must have now.

'Now it isn't for you nor yet for your son, *(whistle)*
But that scolding old wife as you've got at home.'

'Oh take her, oh take her with all of my heart, *(whistle)*
And I wish she and you may never more part.'

So the devil he took the old wife on his back, *(whistle)*
And lugged her along like a pedlar's pack.

He trudged along till he reached his front gate, *(whistle)*
Says: 'Here, take in an old Sussex chap's mate.'

There was thirteen imps all dancing in chains; *(whistle)*
She up with her pattens and beat out their brains.

Two more little devils jumped over the wall, *(whistle)*
Saying: 'Turn her out, father, she'll murder us all.'

So he bundled her up on his back amain, *(whistle)*
And to her old husband he took her again.

'I've been a tormentor the whole of my life, *(whistle)*
But I was never tormented till I met your wife.'

And now to conclude and make an end, *(whistle)*
You see that the women is worse than the men,
If they get sent to Hell, they get kicked back again,
To my fal-de-ral little law-day.

DROYLSDEN WAKES

Sung by Allan Bates, 'heard at Droylsden, Lancs.' (A.G.G. n.d.)

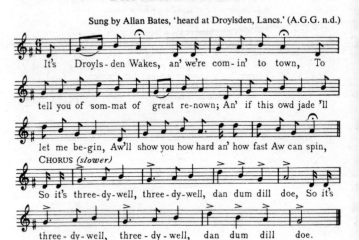

It's Droyls-den Wakes, an' we're com-in' to town, To tell you of som-mat of great re-nown; An' if this owd jade 'll let me be-gin, Aw'll show you how hard an' how fast Aw can spin,

CHORUS (*slower*)

So it's three-dy-well, three-dy-well, dan dum dill doe, So it's three-dy-well, three-dy-well, dan dum dill doe.

Man:　It's Droylsden Wakes, an' we're comin' to town,
　　　　To tell you of sommat of great renown;
　　　　An' if this owd jade'll let me begin,
　　　　Aw'll show you how hard an' how fast Aw can spin,
　　　　　So it's threedywell, threedywell, dan dum dill doe,
　　　　　So it's threedywell, threedywell, dan dum dill doe.

Woman: Thou brags of thysel, but Aw dunno' think it's true,
　　　　For Aw will uphold thee, thy faults aren't a few,
　　　　For when thou has done, an' spun very hard,
　　　　Of this Aw'm well sure, thy work is ill-marred.
　　　　　So it's threedywell, etc.

Man:　Thou saucy owd jade, thou'd best howd thy tongue,
　　　　Or else Aw'll be thumpin' thee ere it be long,
　　　　An' if 'at Aw do, thou'rt sure for to rue,
　　　　For Aw can ha' mony a one's good as you.
　　　　　So it's threedywell, etc.

Woman: What is it to me who you can have?
　　　　Aw shanno' be long ere Aw'm laid i' my grave,
　　　　An' when 'at Aw'm dead, an' ha' done what Aw can,
　　　　You may find one 'at'll spin as hard as Aw've done.
　　　　　So it's threedywell, etc.

THE FALSE BRIDE

Sung by Lucy White, Hambridge, Somerset (C.J.S. 1904)

Oh, when that I saw my love in the_ church stand, With the ring on her fin-ger and the glove in her hand, I jumped in be-twixt them and kissed the false bride, Say-ing: 'A-dieu to false loves for ev-er.'

other verses:

v.3. Al - though she was tied to some oth-er.
v.4. And___ that's the best way to for-get her!

Oh, when that I saw my love in the church stand,
With the ring on her finger and the glove in her hand,
I jumped in betwixt them and kissed the false bride,
Saying: 'Adieu to false loves for ever.'

Oh, when that I saw my love out the church go,
With the bridesmen and bridesmaids they made a fine show,
Then I followed after with my heart full of woe,
For I was the man that ought to had her.

Oh, when that I saw my love sat down to meat,
I sat myself by her but no thing could eat.
I thought her sweet company better than wine,
Although she was tied to some other.

Go dig me a grave both long, wide, and deep,
And strew it all over with flowers so sweet,
That I may lay down there and take my long sleep,
And that's the best way to forget her.

Ralph Vaughan Williams and A. L. Lloyd

FARE THEE WELL, MY DEAREST DEAR

Sung by Mrs Verrall, Horsham, Sussex (R.V.W. 1904)

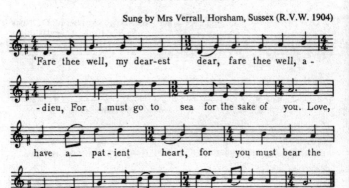

'Fare thee well, my dear-est dear, fare thee well, a-dieu, For I must go to sea for the sake of you. Love, have a— pat-ient heart, for you must bear the smart, Since you and I— must part, my tur-tle dove.'

'Fare thee well, my dearest dear, fare thee well, adieu,
For I must go to sea for the sake of you.
Love, have a patient heart, for you must bear the smart,
Since you and I must part, my turtle dove.

'You'll have silver and bright gold, houses and land,
What more can you desire, love? Don't complain.
And jewels to your hand, and maids at your command,
But you must think of me when I am gone.'

'Your gold I'll count as dust when that you have fled,
Your absence proves me lost and strikes me dead.
And when you are from home, your servants I'll have none.
I'd rather live alone than in company.'

And so nimbly then she dressed all in man's attire,
For to go to sea was her heart's desire.
She cut her lovely hair, and no mistrust was there
That she a maiden were, all at the time.

To Venice we were bound with our hearts content,
No fear of ship being wrecked, away we went.
From London but one day, our ship was cast away,
Which caused our lives to lay in discontent.

Our ship was cast away, misfortune it did frown,
For I did swim to shore, but she was drowned.
Now she lies in the deep, in everlasting sleep,
Which causes me to weep for evermore.

GAOL SONG

Sung by W. Davy, Beaminster, Dorset (H.E.D.H. 1906)

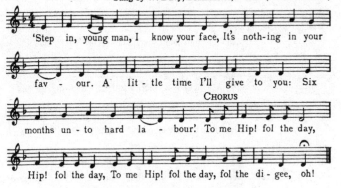

'Step in, young man, I know your face, It's noth-ing in your fav - our. A lit - tle time I'll give to you: Six months un - to hard la - bour.' To me Hip! fol the day, Hip! fol the day, To me Hip! fol the day, fol the di - gee, oh!

CHORUS

'Step in, young man, I know your face,
It's nothing in your favour.
A little time I'll give to you:
Six months unto hard labour.'
    To me Hip! fol the day, Hip! fol the day,
    To my Hip! fol the day, fol the digee, oh!

At six o'clock our turnkey comes in,
With a bunch of keys all in his hand.
'Come, come, my lads, step up and grind.
Tread the wheel till breakfast time.'
    To me Hip! etc.

At eight o'clock our skilly comes in,
Sometimes thick and sometimes thin,
But devil a word we must not say –
It's bread and water all next day.
    To me Hip! etc.

At half past eight the bell doth ring.
Into the chapel we must swing,
'Down on our bended knees to fall.
The Lord have mercy on us all.'
    To me Hip! etc.

At nine o'clock the jangle rings.
All on the trap, boys, we must spring.
'Come, come, my lads, step up in time,
The wheel to tread and the corn to grind.'
    To me Hip! etc.

Now Saturday's come, I'm sorry to say,
Sunday is our starvation day.
Our hobnail boots and tin mugs too,
They are not shined nor they will not do.
    To me Hip! etc.

Now six long months are over and past,
I will return to my bonny bonny lass,
I'll leave the turnkeys all behind,
The wheel to tread and the corn to grind,
    To me Hip! etc.

Ralph Vaughan Williams and A. L. Lloyd

THE GENTLEMAN SOLDIER

Sung by Mr Coomber, Blackham, Sussex (A.G.G. 1907)

It's of a gentleman soldier, as a sentry he did stand,
He kindly saluted a fair maid by waving of his hand.
So boldly then he kissed her, and passed it as a joke.
He drilled her into the sentry-box, wrapped up in a soldier's cloak.

Chorus: For the drums did go with a rap-a-tap-tap,
And the fifes did loudly play,
Saying: 'Fare you well, my Polly dear,
I must be going away.'

Oh, there they tossed and tumbled, till daylight did appear.
The soldier rose, put on his clothes, saying: 'Fare you well, my dear,
For the drums they are a-beating, and the fifes so sweetly play;
If it warn't for that, dear Polly, along with you I'd stay.'
For the drums did go, etc.

38

'Now, come, you gentleman soldier, and won't you marry me?'
'Oh no, my dearest Polly, such things can never be,
For married I am already, and children I have three.
Two wives are allowed in the army, but one's too many for me!'
      For the drums did go, etc.

'If anyone come a-courting you, you treat 'em to a glass.
If anyone come a-courting, you say you're a country lass.
You needn't even tell them that ever you played this joke,
That ever you went in a sentry-box, wrapped up in a soldier's cloak.'
      For the drums did go, etc.

'It's come, my gentleman soldier, why didn't you tell me so?
My parents will be angry when this they come to know.'
When long nine months was up and past, this poor girl she brought shame,
For she had a little militia boy, and she couldn't tell his name.
      For the drums did go, etc.

GEORDIE

Sung by Charles Neville, East Coker, Som. (C.J.S. 1908)

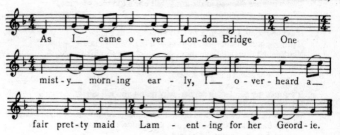

As I came over London Bridge
One misty morning early,
I overheard a fair pretty maid
Lamenting for her Geordie.

As I came over London Bridge
One misty morning early,
I overheard a fair pretty maid
Lamenting for her Geordie.

'Come bridle me my milk-white horse,
Come bridle me my pony,
That I may ride to London's court,
To plead for the life of Geordie.'

And when she entered in the hall,
There was lords and ladies plenty.
Down on her bended knee she fall,
To plead for the life of Geordie.

'Oh, Geordie stole no cow nor calf,
Nor sheep he never stole any,
But he stole sixteen of the king's wild deer,
And sold them in Bohenny.

'Oh, two brave children I've had by him,
And the third lies in my bosom;
And if you would spare my Geordie's life,
I'd freely part from them every one.'

The judge looked over his left shoulder,
And said: 'I'm sorry for thee.
My pretty fair maid, you come too late,
For he's condemned already.'

'Let Geordie hang in golden chains,
Such chains as never was any,
Because he came of the royal blood,
And courted a virtuous lady.

'I wish I was in yonder grove,
Where times I have been many,
With my broad sword and pistol too,
I'd fight for the life of Geordie.'

Ralph Vaughan Williams and A. L. Lloyd

GEORGE COLLINS

Sung by Henry Stansbridge, Lyndhurst, Hants. (G.B.G. 1906)

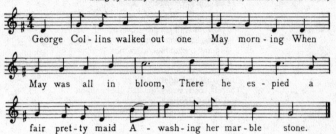

George Collins walked out one May morning
When May was all in bloom, There he espied a
fair pretty maid A-washing her marble stone.

George Collins walked out one May morning
When May was all in bloom.
There he espied a fair pretty maid
A-washing her marble stone.

She whooped, she holloed, she highered her voice,
She held up her lilywhite hand.
'Come hither to me, George Collins,' she said,
'For your life shall not last you long.'

He put his foot on the broad water side,
And over the lea sprung he.
He embraced her around the middle so small,
And kissed her red rosy cheeks.

George Collins rode home to his father's own gate.
'Rise, mother, and make my bed,
And I will trouble my dear sister
For a napkin to tie round my head.

'And if I should chance to die this night,
As I suppose I shall,
Bury me under that marble stone
That's against fair Eleanor's hall.'

Fair Eleanor sat in her room so fine,
Working her silken skein.
She saw the fairest corpse a-coming
That ever the sun shone on.

She said unto her Irish maid:
'Whose corpse is this so fine?'
'This is George Collins' corpse a-coming,
That once was a true lover of thine.'

'Come put him down, my six pretty lads,
And open his coffin so fine,
That I might kiss his lilywhite lips,
For ten thousand times he has kissed mine.

'You go upstairs and fetch me the sheet
That's wove with the silver twine,
And hang that over George Collins' head.
Tomorrow it shall hang over mine.'

The news was carried to London town,
And wrote on London gate,
That six pretty maids died all of one night,
And all for George Collins' sake.

THE GOLDEN VANITY

Sung by W. Bolton, Southport, Lancs. (A.G.G. 1906)

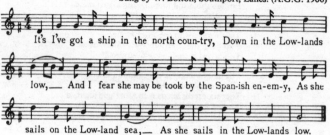

It's I've got a ship in the north country,
Down in the Lowlands low,
And I fear she may be took by the Spanish enemy,
As she sails on the Lowland sea,
As she sails in the Lowlands low.

And up then stepped a little cabin boy,
Down in the Lowlands low,
Saying: 'What'll you give me if I do them destroy,
And sink them in the Lowland sea,
And sink them in the Lowlands low?'

'Oh, I'll give you silver and likewise gold,
Down in the Lowlands low,
And my only daughter for to be your bride,
If you'll sink them in the Lowland sea,
If you'll sink them in the Lowlands low.'

'Oh wrap me up in my black bear skin,
Down in the Lowlands low,
And heave me overboard for to sink or to swim,
And I'll sink them in the Lowland sea,
I'll sink them in the Lowlands low.'

Now some was playing cards and the others playing dice,
Down in the Lowlands low,
And the boy had an auger, bored two holes at once,
And he sunk them in the Lowland sea,
And he sunk them in the Lowlands low.

He leaned upon his breast and he swum back again,
Down in the Lowlands low,
Saying: 'Master, take me up, for I'm sure I will be slain
And I've sunk her in the Lowland sea,
And I've sunk her in the Lowlands low.'

'I'll not take you up,' the master he cried,
  Down in the Lowlands low,
'But I'll shoot you and kill you and send you with the tide,
  And I'll drown you in the Lowland sea,
  And I'll drown you in the Lowlands low.'

He leaned upon his breast and swum round the larboard side,
  Down in the Lowlands low,
'O messmates, take me up for I fear I will be slain,
  And I've sunk her in the Lowland sea,
  And I've sunk her in the Lowlands low.'

His messmates took him up, and on the deck he died,
  Down in the Lowlands low,
And they wrapped him up in an old cow's hide,
  And they sunk him in the Lowland sea,
  And sunk him in the Lowlands low.

THE GREEN BED

Sung by Benjamin Arnold, Easton, nr Winchester (R.V.W. 1909)

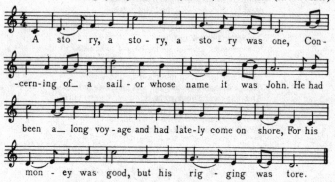

A story, a story, a story was one,
Concerning of a sailor whose name it was John.
He had been a long voyage and had lately come on shore,
For his money was good, but his rigging was tore.

Johnny went to an ale-house where he'd been before,
And he called for a glass of the very best beer.
'You're welcome in, young Johnny, you're welcome in,' said she,
'For last night my daughter Molly was dreaming of thee.'

'What news, my young Johnnie, what news from the sea?
'Bad news,' says young Johnnie, 'for all's gone from me.
Our ship sprung a leak, ma'am, the voyage being crossed,
And on the wide ocean, crew and cargo was lost.

'Call down your daughter Molly and sit her on my knee.
We'll drown all our sorrows and merry we'll be.'
'My daughter Molly's busy, John, and cannot come to you,
And neither would I trust you for one pot nor two.'

Johnny being tired, he hung down his head.
He called for a candle to light him to bed.
'Our beds are all engaged, John, and will be for a week,
So now for fresh lodgings you must go and seek.'

'Oh, what is your reckoning?' the sailor he said.
'Oh what is your reckoning? for you shall be paid.'
'There's forty four shillings, John, you owe me of old.'
Then out of his pocket he drew handfuls of gold.

46

At the sight of this money, the landlady did rue.
'I'll have you remember all I've done for you,
  For what I've just said, John, was all said in jest.
  Of all of my boarders I like you the best.'

At the jingle of his money, young Molly flew downstairs.
She huddled him and cuddled him and called him her dear.
'The green bed is empty, and has been all week,
  Where you and young Molly can take your sweet sleep.'

'Before I would lie in your green bed, I know,
I would rather lie out in the rain and the snow,
For if I'd no money, out of doors I'd be turned,
And it's you and your green bed deserve to be burned.'

Come all you young sailors that sails on the main,
That do get your living in cold storms of rain;
Now, when you have got it, pray lay it up in store,
For the fear that your companions should turn you out of doors.

Ralph Vaughan Williams and A. L. Lloyd

THE GREENLAND WHALE FISHERY

Sung by W. Bolton, Southport, Lancs. (A.G.G. 1906)

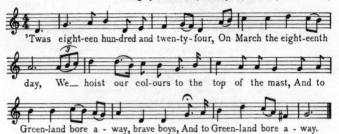

'Twas eight-een hun-dred and twen-ty-four, On March the eight-eenth day, We— hoist our col-ours to the top of the mast, And to Green-land bore a-way, brave boys, And to Green-land bore a-way.

'Twas eighteen hundred and twenty four,
On March the eighteenth day,
We hoist our colours to the top of the mast,
And to Greenland bore away, brave boys,
And to Greenland bore away.

Oh, the look-out up on the mainmast stood
With a spy-glass in his hand.
'There's a whale, there's a whale, and a whale-fish,' he cried,
'And she blows at every span, brave boys,
And she blows at every span.'

The captain stood on the quarterdeck,
And the ice was in his eye.
'Overhaul, overhaul, let your jib-sheet fall,
And put your boats to sea, brave boys,
And put your boats to sea!'

Oh, the boats got down and the men aboard,
And the whale was full in view.
Resolved, resolved was each whalerman bold
To steer where the whale-fish blew, brave boys,
To steer where the whale-fish blew.

Now the harpoon struck and the lines played out,
But she gave such a flourish with her tail,
She capsized our boat and we lost five men,
And we could not catch that whale, brave boys,
And we could not catch that whale.

48

Oh, the losing of that sperm-whale fish
It grieved our captain sore,
But the losing of those five jolly tars,
Oh, it grieved him ten times more, brave boys,
Oh, it grieved him ten times more.*

'Up anchor now,' the captain cried,
'For the winter's star do appear,
It is time for to leave this cold country,
And for England we will steer, brave boys,
And for England we will steer.'

Oh, Greenland is a barren place,
It's a place that bears no green,
Where there's ice and snow, and the whale-fish blow,
And the daylight's seldom seen, brave boys,
And the daylight's seldom seen.

*In some more modern versions, the two sources of grief are put in reverse order.

Ralph Vaughan Williams and A. L. Lloyd

THE GREY COCK OR THE LOVER'S GHOST

Sung by Mrs Cecilia Costello, Birmingham (M.S. & P.S.-S. 1951)

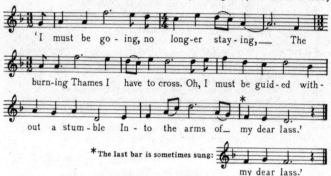

*The last bar is sometimes sung:

'I must be going, no longer staying,
The burning Thames I have to cross.
Oh, I must be guided without a stumble
Into the arms of my dear lass.'

When he came to his true love's window,
He knelt down gently on a stone,
And it's through a pane he whispered slowly:
'My dear girl, are you alone?'

She rose her head from her down-soft pillow,
And snowy were her milk-white breasts,
Saying: 'Who's there, who's there at my bedroom window,
Disturbing me from my long night's rest?'

'Oh, I'm your love and don't discover,*
I pray you rise, love, and let me in,
For I am fatigued from my long night's journey.
Besides, I am wet into the skin.'

Now this young girl rose and put on her clothing.
She quickly let her own true love in.
Oh, they kissed, shook hands, and embraced together,
Till that long night was near an end.

'O Willie dear, O dearest Willie,
Where is that colour you'd some time ago?'
'O Mary dear, the clay has changed me.
I'm but the ghost of your Willie O.'

*Perhaps the phrase should be: 'but I can't uncover' (can't reveal myself).

50

'Then O cock, O cock, O handsome cockerel,
I pray you not crow until it is day.
For your wings I'll make of the very first beaten gold,
And your comb I'll make of the silver grey.'

But the cock it crew, and it crew so fully.
It crew three hours before it was day.
And before it was day, my love had to go away.
Not by the light of the moon or the light of day.

Then it's 'Willie dear, O dearest Willie,
Whenever shall I see you again?'
'When the fish they fly, love, and the sea runs dry, love,
And the rocks they melt in the heat of the sun.'

I WISH, I WISH

Sung by Mrs C. Costello, Birmingham (M.S. and P.S.-S. 1951)

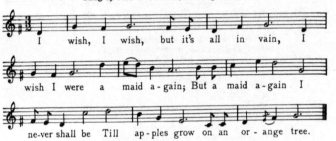

I wish, I wish, but it's all in vain, I wish I were a maid again; But a maid again I never shall be Till apples grow on an orange tree.

I wish, I wish, but it's all in vain,
I wish I were a maid again;
But a maid again I never shall be
Till apples grow on an orange tree.

I wish my baby it was born,
And smiling on its papa's knee,
And I to be in yon churchyard,
With long green grass growing over me.

When my apron-strings hung low,
He followed me through frost and snow,
But now my apron's to my chin,
He passes by and says nothing.

Oh grief, oh grief, I'll tell you why –
That girl has more gold than I;
More gold than I and beauty and fame,
But she will come like me again.

Ralph Vaughan Williams and A. L. Lloyd

JACK THE JOLLY TAR

Sung by Mrs Hooper, Hambridge, Somerset (C.J.S. 1904)

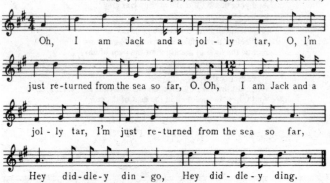

Oh, I am Jack and a jolly tar, O.
I'm just returned from the sea so far, O.
Oh, I am Jack and a jolly tar,
I'm just returned from the sea so far.
  Hey diddley dingo,
  Hey diddley ding.

As Jack was walking through London city,
He heard a squire talking to a lady.
And Jack he heard the squire say:
'Tonight with you, love, I mean to stay.

'You must tie a string all around your finger
With the other end hanging out the window,
And I'll slip by and pull the string
And you must come down and let me in.'

'Damn me,' says Jack, 'if I don't venture
For to pull that string hanging out the window.'
So he slipped by and he pulled the string,
And the lady came down and let him in.

The squire came by all in a passion,
Saying: 'Curse the women throughout the nation!
For here I am, no string I've found,
Behold my hopes all gone aground!'

Early in the morning, the sun was gleaming,
The lady woke up and started screaming,
For there's old Jack in his tarry shirt,
And behold his face all streaked with dirt.

'Oh what is this, you tarry sailor?
 Have you broken in for to steal my treasure?'
'Oh no,' says Jack, 'I just pulled the string,
 And you came down, ma'am, and let me in.'

'Oh,' then says Jack, 'won't you please forgive me?
 I'll steal away so no-one shall see me.'
'Oh no,' says she, 'don't stray too far,
 For I never will part from my jolly Jack Tar.'
   Hey diddley dingo,
   Hey diddley ding.

JOHN BARLEYCORN

Sung by 'Shepherd' Haden, Bampton, Oxon. (C.J.S. 1909)

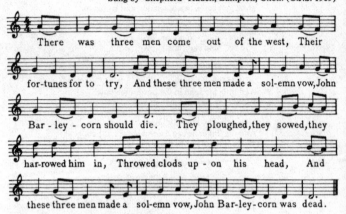

There was three men come out of the west, Their for-tunes for to try, And these three men made a sol-emn vow, John Bar-ley-corn should die. They ploughed, they sowed, they har-rowed him in, Throwed clods up-on his head, And these three men made a sol-emn vow, John Bar-ley-corn was dead.

There was three men came out of the west,
Their fortunes for to try,
And these three men made a solemn vow,
John Barleycorn should die.
They ploughed, they sowed, they harrowed him in,
Throwed clods upon his head,
And these three men made a solemn vow,
John Barleycorn was dead.

Then they let him lie for a very long time
Till the rain from heaven did fall,
Then little Sir John sprung up his head,
And soon amazed them all.
They let him stand till midsummer
Till he looked both pale and wan,
And little Sir John he growed a long beard
And so became a man.

They hired men with the scythes so sharp
To cut him off at the knee,
They rolled him and tied him by the waist,
And served him most barbarously.
They hired men with the sharp pitchforks
Who pricked him to the heart,
And the loader he served him worse than that,
For he bound him to the cart.

They wheeled him round and round the field
Till they came unto a barn,
And there they made a solemn mow
Of poor John Barleycorn.
They hired men with the crab-tree sticks
To cut him skin from bone,
And the miller he served him worse than that,
For he ground him between two stones.

Here's little Sir John in a nut-brown bowl,
And brandy in a glass;
And little Sir John in the nut-brown bowl
Proved the stronger man at last.
And the huntsman he can't hunt the fox,
Nor so loudly blow his horn,
And the tinker he can't mend kettles or pots
Without a little of Barleycorn.

Ralph Vaughan Williams and A. L. Lloyd

LISBON

Sung by Mrs Lock, Muchelney Ham, Somerset (C.J.S. 1904)

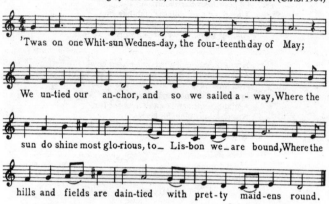

'Twas on one Whit-sun Wednes-day, the four-teenth day of May;
We un-tied our an-chor, and so we sailed a-way, Where the
sun do shine most glo-rious, to Lis-bon we are bound, Where the
hills and fields are dain-tied with pret-ty maid-ens round.

'Twas on one Whitsun Wednesday, the fourteenth day of May,
We untied our anchor, and so we sailed away,
Where the sun do shine most glorious, to Lisbon we are bound,
Where the hills and fields are daintied with pretty maidens round.

I wrote a letter to Nancy, for she to understand
That I was going to leave her, unto some foreign land.
She said: 'My dearest William, those words will break my heart,
Oh, let us married be tonight before that you do start.

'For ten long weeks and better, love, I've been with child by thee,
So stay at home, dear William; be kind and marry me.'
'Our captain has commanded us and I shall have to go.
For the Queen's in want of men, my love, I dare not answer No.'

'Oh, I'll cut off my yellow hair, men's clothing I'll put on,
And I will go along with you and be your waiting man,
And when it is your watch on deck, your duty I will do.
I'd face the field of battle, love, so I could be with you.'

'Your pretty little fingers, they are both long and small.
Your waist it is too slender to face the cannon-ball.
For the cannons loud do rattle and the blazing bullets fly,
And the silver trumpets they do sound to drown the dismal cry.

56

'If I should meet a pretty girl that's proper tall and gay,
 If I should take a fancy to her, Polly, what would you say?
 Would you not be offended?' 'Oh no, my lover true,
 I'd stand aside, sweet William, while she does pleasure you.

'Pray do not talk of danger, for love is my desire,
 To see you in the battle and with you spend my time;
 And I will travel through France and Spain all for to be your bride,
 And within the field of battle I will lay down by your side.'

Ralph Vaughan Williams and A. L. Lloyd

LONG LANKIN

Sung by Sister Emma, Clewer, Berks. (C.J.S. 1909)

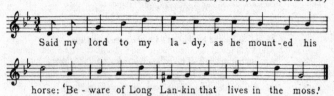

Said my lord to my lady, as he mounted his horse:
'Beware of Long Lankin that lives in the moss.'

Said my lord to my lady, as he rode away:
'Beware of Long Lankin that lives in the hay.

'Let the doors be all bolted and the windows all pinned,
And leave not a hole for a mouse to creep in.'

So he kissed his fair lady and he rode away,
And he was in fair London before the break of day.

The doors were all bolted and the windows all pinned,
Except one little window where Long Lankin crept in.

'Where's the lord of this house?' said Long Lankin.
'He's away in fair London,' said the false nurse to him.

'Where's the little heir of this house?' said Long Lankin.
'He's asleep in his cradle,' said the false nurse to him.

'We'll prick him, we'll prick him all over with a pin,
And that'll make my lady to come down to him.'

So he pricked him, he pricked him all over with a pin,
And the nurse held the basin for the blood to flow in.

'O nurse, how you slumber. O nurse, how you sleep.
You leave my little son Johnson to cry and to weep.

'O nurse, how you slumber, O nurse how you snore.
You leave my little son Johnson to cry and to roar.'

'I've tried him with an apple, I've tried him with a pear.
Come down, my fair lady, and rock him in your chair.

'I've tried him with milk and I've tried him with pap.
Come down, my fair lady, and rock him in your lap.'

58

'How durst I go down in the dead of the night
Where there's no fire a-kindled and no candle alight?'

'You have three silver mantles as bright as the sun.
Come down, my fair lady, all by the light of one.'

My lady came down, she was thinking no harm.
Long Lankin stood ready to catch her in his arm.

Here's blood in the kitchen. Here's blood in the hall.
Here's blood in the parlour where my lady did fall.

Her maiden looked out from the turret so high,
And she saw her master from London riding by.

'O master, O master, don't lay the blame on me.
'Twas the false nurse and Lankin that killed your lady.'

Long Lankin was hung on a gibbet so high
And the false nurse was burnt in a fire close by.

LORD THOMAS AND FAIR ELEANOR

Sung by Mrs Pond, Shepton Beauchamp, Som. (C.J.S. 1904)

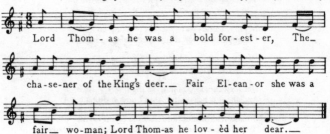

Lord Thom-as he was a bold for-est-er, The
cha-se-ner of the King's deer.— Fair El-ean-or she was a
fair— wo-man; Lord Thom-as he lov-èd her dear.—

Lord Thomas he was a bold forester,
The chasener of the King's deer.
Fair Eleanor she was a fair woman;
Lord Thomas he lovèd her dear.

'Oh riddle, Oh riddle, dear mother,' he said,
'Oh riddle it both as one,
Whether I shall marry fair Ellen or not,
And leave the brown girl alone?'

'The brown girl she've a-got houses and land,
Fair Ellen she've a-got none,
Therefore I charge thee to my blessing
To bring the brown girl home.'

Lord Thomas he went to fair Eleanor's tower.
He knocked so loud on the ring.
There was none so ready as fair Eleanor's self
To let Lord Thomas in.

'What news, what news, Lord Thomas?' she said,
'What news have you brought to me?'
'I've come to invite thee to my wedding
Beneath the sycamore tree.'

'O God forbid, Lord Thomas,' she said,
'That any such thing should be done.
I thought to have been the bride myself,
And you to have been the groom.'

'Oh riddle, Oh riddle, dear mother,' she said,
'Oh riddle it both as one,
Whether I go to Lord Thomas's wedding,
Or better I stay at home?'

'There's a hundred of thy friends, dear child,
A hundred of thy foes,
Therefore I beg thee with all my blessing
To Lord Thomas's wedding don't go.'

But she dressed herself in her best attire,
Her merry men all in green,
And every town that she went through,
They thought she was some queen.

Lord Thomas he took her by the hand,
He led her through the hall,
And he sat her down in the noblest chair
Among the ladies all.

'Is this your bride, Lord Thomas?' she says.
'I'm sure she looks wonderful brown,
When you used to have the fairest young lady
That ever the sun shone on.'

'Despise her not,' Lord Thomas he said,
'Despise her not unto me.
For more do I love your little finger
Than all her whole body.'

This brown girl she had a little pen-knife
Which was both long and sharp.
And betwixt the long ribs and the short
She pricked fair Eleanor's heart.

'Oh, what is the matter?' Lord Thomas he said.
'Oh, can you not very well see?
Can you not see my own heart's blood
Come trickling down my knee?'

Lord Thomas's sword is hung by his side,
As he walked up and down the hall,
And he took off the brown girl's head from her shoulders,
And he flung it against the wall.

He put the handle to the ground,
The sword into his heart.
No sooner did three lovers meet,
No sooner did they part.

Lord Thomas was buried in the church,
Fair Eleanor in the choir,
And out of her bosom there grew a red rose,
And out of Lord Thomas a briar.

And it grew till it reached the church steeple top,
Where it could grow no higher,
And there it entwined like a true lover's knot
For all true loves to admire.

LOVELY JOAN

Sung by C. Jay, Acle, Norfolk (R.V.W. 1908)

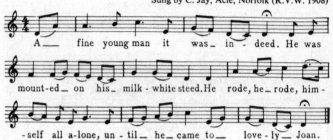

A fine young man it was indeed.
He was mounted on his milk-white steed.
He rode, he rode, himself all alone,
Until he came to lovely Joan.

'Good morning to you, pretty maid.'
And 'Twice good morning, sir,' she said.
He gave her a wink, she rolled her eye.
Says he to himself: 'I'll be there by and by.'

'Oh, don't you think these pooks of hay
A pretty place for us to play?
So come with me like a sweet young thing,
And I'll give you my golden ring.'

Then he pulled off his ring of gold.
'My pretty little miss, do this behold.
I'd freely give it for your maidenhead.'
And her cheeks they blushed like the roses red.

'Give me that ring into my hand,
And I will neither stay nor stand,
For this would do more good to me
Than twenty maidenheads,' said she.

And as he made for the pooks of hay,
She leaped on his horse and tore away.
He called, he called, but it was all in vain;
Young Joan she never looked back again.

She didn't think herself quite safe,
No, not till she came to her true love's gate.
She's robbed him of his horse and ring,
And left him to rage in the meadows green.

LUCY WAN

Sung by Mrs Dann, Cottenham, Cambs. (E.B. & W.P.M. n.d.)

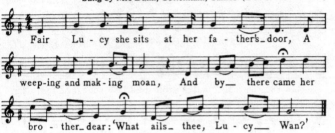

Fair Lucy she sits at her father's door,
A-weeping and making moan,
And by there came her brother dear:
'What ails thee, Lucy Wan?'

'I ail, and I ail, dear brother,' she said,
'I'll tell you the reason why;
There is a child between my two sides,
Between you, dear Billy, and I.'

And he has drawn his good broad sword,
That hung down by his knee,
And he has cutted off Lucy Wan's head,
And her fair body in three.

'Oh, I have cutted off my greyhound's head,
And I pray you pardon me.'
'Oh, this is not the blood of our greyhound,
But the blood of our Lucy.'

'Oh, what shall you do when your father comes to know?
My son, pray tell unto me.'
'I shall dress myself in a new suit of blue
And sail to some far country.'

'Oh, what will you do with your houses and your lands?
My son, pray tell unto me?'
'Oh, I shall leave them all to my children so small,
By one, by two, by three.'

'Oh, when shall you turn to your own wife again?
My son, pray tell unto me.'
'When the sun and the moon rise over yonder hill,
And I hope that may never, never be.'

THE MANCHESTER 'ANGEL'

Sung by S. Gregory, Beaminster, Dorset (H.E.D.H. 1906)

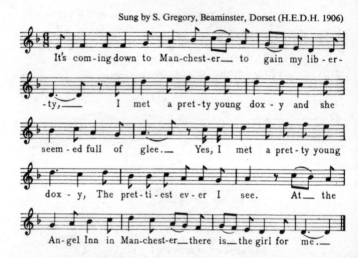

It's coming down to Manchester to gain my liberty,
I met a pretty young doxy and she seemed full of glee.
Yes, I met a pretty young doxy, the prettiest ever I see.
At the Angel Inn in Manchester, there is the girl for me.

Then early next morning, just at the break of day,
I went to my love's bedside, my morning vows to pay.
I hugged her, I cuddled her, I bade her to lie warm;
And she said: 'My jolly soldier, do you mean me any harm?'

'To mean you any harm, my love, is a thing that I would scorn.
If I stopped along with you all night, I'd marry you in the morn.
Before my lawful officer, my vows I will fulfil.'
Then she said: 'My jolly soldier, you may lie as long as you will.'

Our rout came on the Thursday, on the Monday we marched away.
The drums and fifes and bugles so sweetly did play.
Some hearts they were merry, but mine was full of woe.
She says: 'May I go along with you?' 'Oh no, my love, oh no.

'If you should stand on sentry go, on a cold and bitter day,
Your colours they would go, love, and your beauty would decay.
If I saw you handle a musket, love, it would fill my heart with woe
So stay at home, dear Nancy.' But still she answered: 'No.

'I'll go down to your officer, and I'll buy your discharge,
Ten guineas I'll surrender if they'll set you at large.
And if that will not do, my love, along with you I'll go,
So will you take me with you now?' And still I answered: 'No.'

'I'll go down in some nunnery and there I'll end my life.
I'll never have no lover now, nor yet become a wife.
But constant and true-hearted, love, for ever I'll remain,
And I never will get married till my soldier comes again!'

Ralph Vaughan Williams and A. L. Lloyd

THE MAN OF BURNINGHAM TOWN

Sung by Mr Locke, Rollesby, Norfolk (R.V.W. 1908)

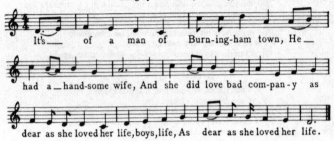

It's of a man of Burningham town, He had a handsome wife, And she did love bad company as dear as she loved her life, boys, life, As dear as she loved her life.

It's of a man of Burningham town,
He had a handsome wife,
And she did love bad company
As dear as she loved her life, boys, life,
As dear as she loved her life.

Now this poor man would go to sea,
His living for to get.
Where he made one penny, she spent two.
It was all for want of wit, boys, wit,
It was all for want of wit.

Now this poor man came home from sea,
It being all late in the night,
He enquired after his own dear wife,
His joy and his heart's delight, boys, light,
His joy and his heart's delight.

Oh, the servant girl she made this reply,
With a voice so wonderful strong:
'She's gone unto the neighbour's house,
And I think she may tarry there long, boys, long,
And I think she may tarry there long.

'Oh, shall I go and fetch her home?'
The poor man begun for to think.
'Oh no,' says he, 'I'll go there myself,
For I think I could do with a drink, boys, drink,
For I think I could do with a drink.'

Now, as he was a-going along of the road,
He heard such a wonderful noise.
And who should it be but his own dear wife,
Along with the Burningham boys, brave boys,
Along with the Burningham boys.

He heard her say: 'Fetch us another full glass,
And I will sit down on your knee,
And we'll fairly well make this old tavern to roar
While our husbands are on the sea, boys, sea,
While our husbands are on the sea.'

This poor man he stood at the door in a maze;
His heart it was very nigh broke,
Then he went back home and he sent out the maid,
While he prepared a rope, boys, rope,
While he prepared a rope.

Then she came a-jumping and skipping in,
Gave him such a joyful kiss,
Saying: 'You're welcome home, my kind husband so dear.
Long time you have been missed, boys, missed,
Long time you have been missed.'

He beat her once, he beat her twice,
Till she was wonderful sore;
And she cries out: 'Oh, my husband dear,
I'll never do the likes any more, boys, more,
I'll never do the likes any more.'

So come all you girls of Burningham town,
A warning take by me;
And don't you spend your money to waste,
While your husband is on the sea, the sea,
While your husband is on the sea.

For if you do they'll make you rue,
And curse the hour you were born,
For the cuckolding of your husband dear,
They'll make you wear the horn, boys, horn,
They'll make you wear the horn.

THE MERMAID

Sung by James Herridge, Twyford, Hants. (E.T.S. 1906)

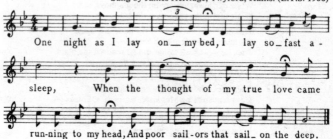

One night as I lay on my bed, I lay so fast asleep, When the thought of my true love came running to my head, And poor sailors that sail on the deep.

One night as I lay on my bed,
I lay so fast asleep,
When the thought of my true love came running to my head,
And poor sailors that sail on the deep.

As I sailed out one day, one day,
And being not far from land,
And there I spied a mermaid a-sitting on a rock,
With a comb and a glass in her hand.

The song she sang, she sang so sweet,
But no answer at all could us make,
Till at length our gallant ship, she tooked round about,
Which made all our poor hearts to ache.

Then up stepped the helmsman of our ship,
In his hand a lead and line,
All for to sound the seas, my boys, that is so wide and deep,
But no hard rock or sand could he find.

Then up stepped the captain of our ship,
And a well-speaking man is he.
He says: 'I have a wife, my boys, in fair Plymouth town,
But this night and a widow she will be.'

Then up stepped the bosun of our ship,
And a well-spoken man was he.
He says: 'I have two sons, my boys, in fair Bristol town,
And orphans I fear they will be.'

And then up stepped the little cabin boy,
And a pretty boy was he.
He says: 'Oh, I grieve for my own mother dear,
Whom I shall nevermore see.

'Last night, when the moon shined bright,
My mother had sons five,
But now she may look in the salt salt seas
And find but one alive.'

Call a boat, call a boat, my fair Plymouth boys,
Don't you hear how the trumpets sound?
For the want of a long-boat in the ocean we were lost,
And the most of our merry men drowned.

MOTHER, MOTHER, MAKE MY BED

Sung by Mrs Ford, Blackham, Sussex (A.G.G. 1906)

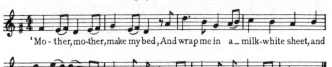

'Mo - ther, mo-ther, make my bed, And wrap me in a _ milk-white sheet, and

wrap me in _ a cloak _ of gold, And see whe-ther I can sleep.'

'Mother, mother, make my bed,
And wrap me in a milk-white sheet,
And wrap me in a cloak of gold,
And see whether I can sleep.

'And send me the two bailies,
Likewise my sister's son,
That they may fetch me my own true love,
Or I shall die before ever he can come.'

The first three miles they walked,
The next three miles they ran,
Until they came to the high water side,
And laid on their breast and swam.

They swam till they came to the high castle
Where my lord he was sitting at meat:
'If you did but know what news I brought,
Not one mouthful more would you eat.'

'What news, what news have you brought me?
Is my castle burnt down?' [me?
'Oh no, your true love is very, very ill,
And she'll die before ever you can come.'

'Saddle me my milk-white horse,
And bridle him so neat,
That I may kiss of her lily lips
That are to me so sweet.'

They saddled him his milk-white steed
At twelve o'clock at night.
He rode, he rode till he met six young men
With a corpse all dressed in white.

'Come set her down, come set her down,
Come set her down by me,
That I may kiss of her lily, lily lips,
Before she is taken away.'

My lady, she died on the Saturday night
Before the sun went down.
My lord he died on the Sunday following
Before evening prayers began.

My lady she was buried in the high castle
My lord was buried in the choir;
Out of my lady grew a red rose,
And out of my lord a sweet briar.

This rose and the briar they grew up together,
Till they could grow no higher,
They met at the top in a true lover's knot,
And the rose it clung round the sweet briar.

THE NEW YORK TRADER

Sung by Ted Goffin, Catfield, Norfolk (E.J.M. 1921)

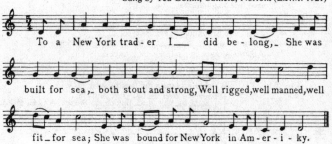

To a New York trad-er I_ did be-long,_ She was
built for sea,_ both stout and strong, Well rigged, well manned, well
fit_for sea; She was bound for New York in Am-er-i-ky.

To a New York trader I did belong,
She was built for sea, both stout and strong,
Well rigged, well manned, well fit for sea;
She was bound for New York in Ameriky.

Our cruel captain, as we did find,
Left half of our provisions behind.
Our cruel captain, as we understand,
Meant to starve us all before we made the land.

At length our hunger grew very great.
We had but little on board to eat,
And we were in necessity,
All by our captain's cruelty.

Our captain in his cabin lay.
A voice came to him and thus did say:
'Prepare yourself and ship's company,
For tomorrow night you shall lay with me.'

Our captain woke in a terrible fright,
It being the first watch of the night,
Aloud for his bo'sun he did call,
And to him related the secret all.

'Bo'sun,' said he, 'it grieves my heart
To think I have acted a villain's part,
To take what was not my lawful due,
To starve the passengers and the ship's crew.

'There is one thing more I have to tell –
When I in Waterford town did dwell,
I killed my master, a merchant there,
All for the sake of his lady fair.

'I killed my wife and children three,
All through that cursed jealousy,
And on my servant I laid the blame,
And hanged he was all for the same.'

'Captain,' said he, 'if that be so,
Pray let none of your ship's crew know,
But keep your secret within your breast,
And pray to God to give you rest.'

Early next morning a storm did rise,
Which our seamen did much surprise;
The sea was over us, both fore and aft,
Till scarce a man on deck was left.

Then the bo'sun he did declare
That our captain was a murderer.
It so enraged the whole ship's crew
They overboard their captain threw.

When this was done a calm was there,
Our good little ship homeward did steer,
The wind abated and calmed the sea,
And we sailed safe to Ameriky.

And when we came to anchor there,
Our good little ship for to repair,
The people wondered much to see
What a poor distressed shipwrecked crew were we.

Ralph Vaughan Williams and A. L. Lloyd

O SHEPHERD, O SHEPHERD

Sung by Mrs Davis, Dorchester, Dorset (H.E.D.H. 1906)

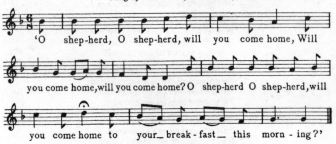

'O shepherd, O shepherd, will you come home, Will you come home, will you come home? O shepherd O shepherd, will you come home to your breakfast this morning?'

'O shepherd, O shepherd, will you come home,
Will you come home, will you come home?
O shepherd, O shepherd, will you come home
To your breakfast this morning?'

'What have you got for my breakfast,
For my breakfast, for my breakfast?
What have you got for my breakfast
If I do come home this morning?'

'Bacon and beans a bellyful,
A bellyful, a bellyful.
Bacon and beans a bellyful
If you do come home this morning.'

'My sheep they are all in the wilderness,
The wilderness, the wilderness.
My sheep they are all in the wilderness
So I cannot come home this morning.'

'O shepherd, O shepherd, will you come home,
Will you come home, will you come home?
O shepherd, O shepherd will you come home
To your dinner this morning?'

'What have you got for my dinner,
For my dinner, for my dinner?
What have you got for my dinner
If I do come home this morning?'

'Pudding and beef a bellyful,
A bellyful, a bellyful.
Pudding and beef a bellyful
If you do come home this morning.'

'My sheep they are all in the wilderness,
The wilderness, the wilderness.
My sheep they are all in the wilderness,
So I cannot come home this morning.'

'O shepherd, O shepherd, will you come home,
Will you come home, will you come home?
O shepherd, O shepherd, will you come home
To your supper tonight?'

'What have you got for my supper,
For my supper, for my supper?
What have you got for my supper
If I do come home tonight?'

'Bread and cheese a bellyful,
A bellyful, a bellyful.
Bread and cheese a bellyful
If you do come home tonight.'

'My sheep they are all in the wilderness,
The wilderness, the wilderness.
My sheep they are all in the wilderness,
So I cannot come home tonight.'

'O shepherd, O shepherd, will you come home,
Will you come home, will you come home?
O shepherd, O shepherd, will you come home
To your lodging tonight?'

'What have you got for my lodging,
For my lodging, for my lodging?
What have you got for my lodging
If I do come home tonight?'

'A clean pair of sheets and a pretty lass,
A pretty lass, a pretty lass.
A clean pair of sheets and a pretty lass,
If you do come home tonight.'

'Oh, I'll drive my sheep out of the wilderness,
The wilderness, the wilderness.
I'll drive my sheep out of the wilderness,
And I will come home tonight!'

Ralph Vaughan Williams and A. L. Lloyd

THE OLD MAN FROM LEE

Sung by unnamed singer, Coggeshall, Essex (G.E.McC. n.d.)

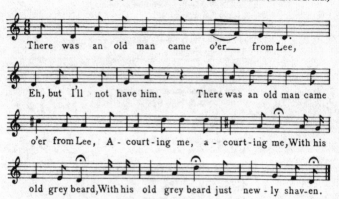

There was an old man came o'er— from Lee,
Eh, but I'll not have him. There was an old man came
o'er from Lee, A - court - ing me, a - court - ing me, With his
old grey beard, With his old grey beard just new - ly shav - en.

There was an old man came o'er from Lee,
Eh, but I'll not have him.
There was an old man came o'er from Lee,
A-courting me, a-courting me,
With his old grey beard,
With his old grey beard
Just newly shaven.

My mother she told me to get him some pie.
Eh, but I'll not have him.
My mother she told me to get him some pie,
I got him some pie and he put the crust by,
With his old grey beard, etc.

My mother she told me to hand him a stool.
Eh, but I'll not have him.
My mother she told me to hand him a stool.
I hand him a stool, he sat down like a fool,
With his old grey beard, etc.

My mother she told me to give him some wine,
Eh, but I'll not have him.
My mother she told me to give him some wine.
I gave him some wine and he drank like a swine,
With his old grey beard, etc.

My mother she told me to take him to church.
Eh, but I'll not have him.
My mother she told me to take him to church.
I took him to church but left him in the lurch,
With his old grey beard, etc.

My mother she told me to take him to bed.
Eh, but I'll not have him.
My mother she told me to take him to bed.
I took him to bed, and he asked me to wed,
With his old grey beard, etc.

Ralph Vaughan Williams and A. L. Lloyd

ON MONDAY MORNING

Sung by W. Alexander, Cliddesdon, Hants (R.V.W. 1909)

On Monday morn-ing I mar-ried a wife, Think-ing to live and a so-ber life, But as she turned out, I'd bet-ter been dead, The re-mark-a-ble day that I was wed, To me rite fol-lol-lid-dle-lol-le-day.

On Monday morning I married a wife,
Thinking to live and a sober life,
But as she turned out, I'd better been dead,
The remarkable day that I was wed,
To me rite fol-lol-liddle-lol-le-day.

On Tuesday morning I goes to the wood,
I cut a stick both fine and good,
The finest stick that ever you did see,
I cut him out of a holly holly tree,
To me rite fol-lol-liddle-lol-le-day.

On Wednesday morning then home goes I,
Thinking a battle I must try.
I beat him about her back and her wig,
Until I'd a-broke me holly, holly twig,
To me rite fol-lol-liddle-lol-le-day.

On Thursday morning my poor wife,
She was sick and like to die,
If she isn't better tomorrow, you see,
The devil may have her for all of me,
To me rite fol-lol-liddle-lol-le-day.

On Friday morning the sun did shine,
And I walked out in the midst of my prime,
Oh, the devil he come in, in the midst of the game,
And he took her away, both blind and lame,
To me rite fol-lol-liddle-lol-le-day.

On Saturday morning it's five days past,
My poor wife is dead at last.
The big bell shall ring and the little one shall toll,
And I'll go home like a jolly old soul,
To my rite fol-lol-liddle-lol-le-day.

On Sunday morning I dined without.
I had ne'er a wife to scold me about.
Here's good luck to my pipe, my bottle, and my friend,
And here's good luck to a week's work's end,
To my rite fol-lol-liddle-lol-le-day.

ONE NIGHT AS I LAY ON MY BED

Sung by Mrs Russell, Upwey, Dorset (H.E.D.H. 1907)

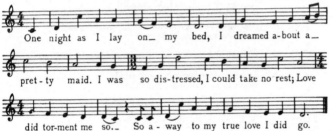

One night as I lay on my bed, I dreamed a-bout a pret-ty maid. I was so dis-tressed, I could take no rest; Love did tor-ment me so. So a-way to my true love I did go.

One night as I lay on my bed,
I dreamed about a pretty maid.
I was so distressed, I could take no rest;
Love did torment me so.
So away to my true love I did go.

But when I came to my love's window,
I boldly called her by her name,
Saying: 'It was for your sake I'm come here so late,
Through this bitter frost and snow.
So it's open the window, my love, do.'

'My mum and dad they are both awake,
And they will sure for to hear us speak.
There'll be no excuse then but sore abuse,
Many a bitter word and blow.
So begone from my window, my love, do.'

'Your mum and dad they are both asleep,
And they are sure not to hear us speak,
For they're sleeping sound on their bed of down,
And they draw their breath so low.
So open the window, my love, do.'

My love arose and she opened the door,
And just like an angel she stood on the floor.
Her eyes shone bright like the stars at night,
And no diamonds could shine so.
So in with my true love I did go.

Ralph Vaughan Williams and A. L. Lloyd

THE OUTLANDISH KNIGHT

Sung by Mr Hilton, South Walsham, Norfolk (R.V.W. 1908)

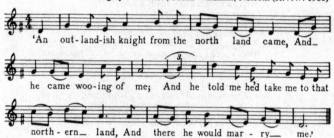

'An out-land-ish knight from the north land came, And he came woo-ing of me; And he told me he'd take me to that north-ern land, And there he would mar-ry me.'

'An outlandish knight from the north land came,
And he came wooing of me;
And he told me he'd take me to that northern land,
And there he would marry me.'

'Well, go and get me some of your father's gold,
And some of your mother's fee,
And two of the very best stable steeds,
Where there stand thirty and three.'

She borrowed some of her father's gold,
And some of her mother's fee,
And away they did go to the stable door,
Where horses stood thirty and three.

She mounted on her lilywhite horse,
And he upon the grey,
And away they did ride to the fair river side,
Three hours before it was day.

He says: 'Unlight, my little Polly,
Unlight, unlight,' cries he,
'For six pretty maids I've drowned here before,
And the seventh thou art to be.

'Pull off, pull off your silken gown,
And deliver it unto me,
For I think it's too fine and much too gay
To rot in the salt water sea.'

She said: 'Go get a sickle to crop the thistle
That grows beside the brim,
That it may not mingle with my curly locks,
Nor harm my lilywhite skin.'

78

So he got a sickle to crop the thistle,
That grew beside the brim,
She catched him around the middle so small,
And tumbled him into the stream.

'Lie there, lie there, you false-hearted man,
Lie there instead of me,
For six pretty maidens thou has drowned here before,
And the seventh has drowned thee.'

Then she mounted on her lilywhite horse,
And she did ride away,
And she arrived at her father's stable door
Three hours before it was day.

Now the parrot being in the window so high,
A-hearing the lady, he did say:
'I'm afraid that some ruffian have led you astray,
That you've tarried so long away.'

'Don't prittle, don't prattle, my pretty Polly,
Nor tell no tales of me,
And your cage shall be of the glittering gold,
And your perch of the best ivory.'

Now the master being in the bedroom so high,
A-hearing the parrot he did say:
'What's the matter with you, my pretty Polly,
You're prattling so long before day?'

'There come an old cat on top of my cage,
To take my sweet life away.
I was just calling on my young mistress
To drive that old puss away.'

T'OWD YOWE WI' ONE HORN

Sung by Dean Robinson, Scawby Brook, Lincs. (P.G. 1905)

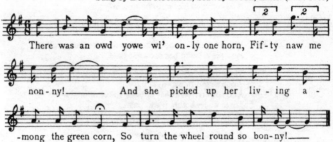

There was an owd yowe wi' on-ly one horn, Fif-ty naw me non-ny!____ And she picked up her liv-ing a-mong the green corn, So turn the wheel round so bon-ny!____

There was an owd yowe wi' only one horn,
    Fifty naw me nonny!
And she picked up her living among the green corn,
    So turn the wheel round so bonny!

One day said the pindar to his man,
    'Oh dear, Johnny!
I prithee go pen that owd yowe if tha can.'
    So turn the wheel round so bonny!

So off went the man to pen this owd yowe,
    Fifty naw me nonny!
She knocked him three times among the green corn,
    So turn the wheel round so bonny!

Then the butcher was sent for to take this yowe's life,
    Fifty naw me nonny!
And along come the butcher a-whetting his knife,
    So turn the wheel round so bonny!

The owd yowe she started a-whetting her pegs,
    Fifty naw me nonny!
She run at the butcher and broke both his legs,
    So turn the wheel round so bonny!

This owd yowe was sent to fight for the king,
    Fifty naw me nonny!
She killed horsemen and footmen just as they came in,
    So turn the wheel round so bonny!

OXFORD CITY

Sung by Mr Harper, King's Lynn, Norfolk (R.V.W. 1905)

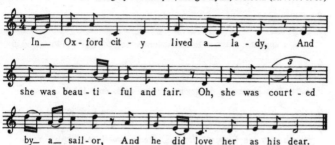

In Oxford city lived a lady,
And she was beautiful and fair.
Oh, she was courted by a sailor,
And he did love her as his dear.

He said: 'My dear, let us get married,
Let us now no longer stay.
I'll work for you both late and early
If you my wedded bride will be.'

This girl she loved him, but at a distance.
She did not seem to be quite so fond.
He said: 'My dear, you seem to slight me.
I'm sure you love some other man.'

He saw her dancing with some other.
A jealous thought came to his mind;
And to destroy his own true lover,
He gave to her a glass of wine.

So soon she drank it, so soon she felt it.
'Oh, hold me fast, my dear,' said she.
'Is it that glass of wine you gave me
That takes my innocent life away?'

'That glass of wine now which I gave you,
That glass of wine did strong poison hide,
For if you won't be my true lover,
You'll never be no other man's bride.

'That glass of wine now which I gave you,
Oh, I have drinked of the same,' said he.
'So in each other's arms we'll die together,
To warn young men of jealousy.'

'Oh hark, oh hark, the cocks are crowing.
The daylight now will soon appear,
And into my cold grave I'm going,
And it's you, Willie, as called me there.'

Ralph Vaughan Williams and A. L. Lloyd

THE PLOUGHMAN

Sung by Henry Burstow, Horsham, Sussex (R.V.W. 1904)

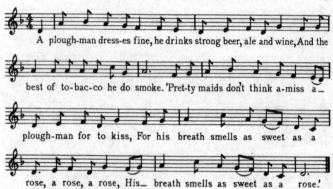

A plough-man dress-es fine, he drinks strong beer, ale and wine, And the best of to-bac-co he do smoke. 'Pret-ty maids don't think a-miss a plough-man for to kiss, For his breath smells as sweet as a rose, a rose, a rose, His breath smells as sweet as a rose.'

A ploughman dresses fine, he drinks strong beer, ale, and wine,
And the best of tobacco he do smoke.
'Pretty maids don't think amiss a ploughman for to kiss,
For his breath smells as sweet as a rose, a rose, a rose,
His breath smells as sweet as a rose.'

A ploughman in his shirt he completely does his work,
And so loudly to the little boy do call,
Saying: 'Be nimble and be quick by the swishing of your whip.'
And so merrily he'll rattle them along, along, along,
And so merrily he'll rattle them along.

When our shears are shod, to the blacksmith off we wad,
And so loudly to the blacksmith we do call,
Saying: 'Be nimble and be quick, and throw your blows in thick.'
And so merrily he will swing his hammer round, around, around,
And so merrily he'll swing his hammer round.

When our shears are done, to the ale-house we will run,
And so loudly to the landlord we do call;
Saying: 'Bring to us some beer, for while I am here,
A ploughman is always a-dry, a-dry, a-dry,
A ploughman is always a-dry.'

RATCLIFFE HIGHWAY

Sung by Mrs Howard, King's Lynn, Norfolk (R.V.W. 1905)

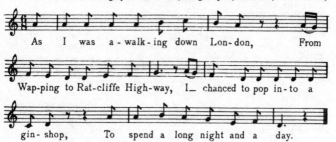

As I was a-walking down London, From
Wapping to Ratcliffe Highway, I chanced to pop into a
gin-shop, To spend a long night and a day.

As I was a-walking down London,
From Wapping to Ratcliffe Highway,
I chanced to pop into a gin-shop,
To spend a long night and a day.

A young doxy came rolling up to me,
And asked if I'd money to sport.
For a bottle of wine changed a guinea,
And she quickly replied: 'That's the sort.'

When the bottle was put on the table,
There was glasses for everyone.
When I asked for the change of my
   guinea,
She tipped me a verse of her song.

This lady flew into a passion,
And placed both her hands on her hip,
Saying: 'Sailor, don't you know our
   fashion?
Do you think you're on board of your
   ship?'

'If this is your fashion to rob me,
Such a fashion I'll never abide.
So launch out the change of my guinea,
Or else I'll give you a broadside.'

A gold watch hung over the mantel,
So the change of my guinea I take,
And down the stairs I run nimbly,
Saying: 'Darn my old boots, I'm
   well paid.'

The night being dark in my favour,
To the river I quickly did creep,
And I jumped in a boat bound for
   Deptford,
And got safe aboard of my ship.

So come all you bold young sailors,
That ramble down Ratcliffe Highway,
If you chance to pop into a gin-shop,
Beware, lads, how long you do stay.

For the songs and the liquors invite you,
And your heart will be all in a rage;
If you give them a guinea for a bottle,
You can go to the devil for change.

83

THE RED HERRING

Sung by Mr Trump, North Petherton, Somerset (C.J.S. 1906)

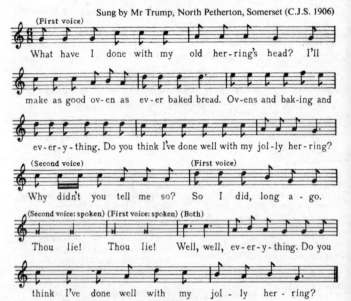

(First voice)

What have I done with my old her-ring's head? I'll make as good ov-en as ev-er baked bread. Ov-ens and bak-ing and ev-er-y-thing. Do you think I've done well with my jol-ly her-ring?

(Second voice) (First voice)

Why didn't you tell me so? So I did, long a-go.

(Second voice: spoken) (First voice: spoken) (Both)

Thou lie! Thou lie! Well, well, ev-er-y-thing. Do you think I've done well with my jol-ly her-ring?

What have I done with my old herring's head?
I'll make as good oven as ever baked bread.
Ovens and baking and everything.
Do you think I've done well with my jolly herring?
      2nd Voice: Why didn't you tell me so?
      1st Voice: So I did, long ago.
(*Spoken*) *2nd Voice:* Thou lie!
(*Spoken*) *1st Voice:* Thou lie!
Well, well, everything.
Do you think I've done well with my jolly herring?

What have I made with my old herring's eyes?
Forty jackdaws and fifty magpies,
Linnets and larks and everything.
Do you think I've done well with my jolly herring?

What have I made of my old herring's ribs?
Blooming great tower and a blooming great bridge.
Bridges, towers, and everything.
Do you think I've done well with my jolly herring?

What have I made of my old herring's guts?
Forty bright women and fifty bright sluts,
Wantons and sluts and everything.
Do you think I've done well with my jolly herring?

What have I made of my old herring's navel?
As good a wheelbarrow as ever drawed gravel,
Wheelbarrow, shovel, and everything.
Do you think I've done well with my jolly herring?

What have I made of my old herring's tail?
I'll make as good ship as ever set sail,
Sailcloth, rigging, and everything.
Do you think I've done well with my jolly herring?

Ralph Vaughan Williams and A. L. Lloyd

ROBIN HOOD AND THE PEDLAR

Sung by Mr Verrall, Horsham, Sussex (R.V.W. 1906)

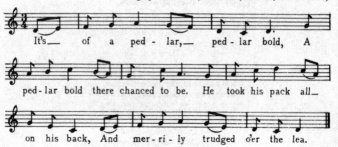

It's___ of a ped‑lar,___ ped‑lar bold, A ped‑lar bold there chanced to be. He took his pack all___ on his back, And mer‑ri‑ly trudged o'er the lea.

It's of a pedlar, pedlar bold
A pedlar bold there chanced to be.
He took his pack all on his back,
And merrily trudged o'er the lea.

By chance he met two troublesome men,
Two troublesome men they chanced to be;
The one of them was bold Robin Hood,
And the other was Little John so free.

'O pedlar, pedlar, what's in thy pack?
Come speedily and tell to me.'
'I've several suits of the gay green cloth,
And silken bowstrings by two and three.'

'If you've several suits of the gay green cloth,
And silken bowstrings two or three,
Then by my body,' cries Little John,
'One half your pack shall belong to me.'

'Oh no, oh no,' says the pedlar bold,
'Oh no, oh no, that never can be,
For there's never a man from fair Nottingham
Can take one half my pack from me.'

Then the pedlar he pulled off his pack,
And put it a little below his knee,
Saying: 'If you do move me one perch from this,
My pack and all shall go with thee.'

Then Little John he drew his sword,
The pedlar by his pack did stand,
They fought until they both did sweat,
And John cried: 'Pedlar, pray hold your hand.'

Then Robin Hood he was standing by,
  And he did laugh most heartily,
'I could find a man of smaller scale,
  Could thrash the pedlar and also thee.'

'Go you try, master,' says Little John,
  'And go you try most speedily,
  For by my body,' says Little John,
'I'm sure this night you will know me.'

Then Robin Hood he drew his sword,
  And the pedlar by his pack did stand;
  They fought till the blood in streams did flow,
Till he cried: 'Pedlar, pray hold your hand.

'Oh pedlar, pedlar, what is thy name?
  Come speedily and tell to me.'
'Well now, my name I never will tell
  Till both your names you have told me.'

'The one of us is bold Robin Hood,
  And the other is Little John so free.'
'Now,' says the pedlar, 'it lays to my good will
  Whether my name I choose to tell thee.

'I'm Gamble Gold of the gay green woods,
  And travelled far beyond the sea.
  For killing a man in my father's land,
  Far from my country I was forced to flee.'

'If you're Gamble Gold of the gay green woods,
  And travelled far beyond the sea,
  You are my mother's own sister's son,
  What nearer cousins can we be?'

They sheathed their swords with friendly words,
  So merrily they did agree.
  They went to a tavern and there they dined,
  And crackèd bottles most merrily.

ROUNDING THE HORN

Sung by W. Bolton, Southport, Lancs. (A.G.G. May 1907)

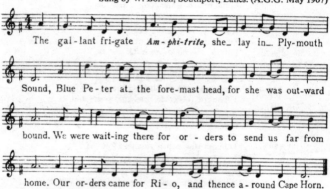

The gal-lant fri-gate *Am-phi-trite*, she_ lay in_ Ply-mouth
Sound, Blue Pe-ter at_ the fore-mast head, for she was out-ward
bound. We were wait-ing there for or - ders to send us far from
home. Our or-ders came for Ri - o, and thence a - round Cape Horn.

The gallant frigate *Amphitrite*, she lay in Plymouth Sound,
Blue Peter at the fore-mast head, for she was outward bound.
We were waiting there for orders to send us far from home.
Our orders came for Rio, and thence around Cape Horn.

When we arrived at Rio, we prepared for heavy gales;
We set up all our rigging, boys, and bent on all new sails.
From ship to ship they cheered us as we did sail along,
And wished us pleasant weather in rounding of Cape Horn.

When beating off Magellan Straits it blew exceeding hard,
While shortening sail, two gallant tars fell from the tops'l yard.
By angry seas the ropes we threw from their poor hands was torn,
We were forced to leave them to the sharks that prowl around Cape Horn.

When we got round the Horn, my boys, we had some glorious days,
And very soon our killick dropped in Valparaiso Bay.
The pretty girls came down in flocks, I solemnly declare
They're far before the Plymouth girls with their long and curly hair.

They love a jolly sailor when he spends his money free;
They'll laugh and sing and merry, merry be, and have a jovial spree.
And when your money is all gone, they won't on you impose;
They are not like the Plymouth girls that'll pawn and sell your clothes.

Farewell to Valparaiso, and farewell for a while.
Likewise to all the Spanish girls along the coast of Chile.
And if ever I live to be paid off, I'll sit and sing this song:
'God bless those pretty Spanish girls we left around Cape Horn.'

THE ROYAL OAK

Sung by Moses Mansfield, Haslemere, Surrey (C.C. 1912)

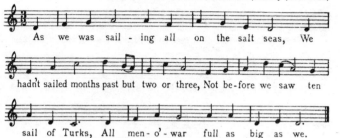

As we was sail - ing all on the salt seas, We hadn't sailed months past but two or three, Not be-fore we saw ten sail of Turks, All men - o' - war full as big as we.

As we was sailing all on the salt seas,
We hadn't sailed months past but two or three,
Not before we saw ten sail of Turks,
All men-o'-war full as big as we.

'Pull down your colours, you English dogs!
Pull down your colours, do not refuse.
Oh, pull down your colours, you English dogs,
Or else your precious life you'll lose!'

Our captain being a valiant man,
And a well-bespoken young man were he:
'Oh, it never shall be said that we died like dogs,
But we will fight them most manfully!

'Go up, you lofty cabin boys,
And mount the mainmast topsail high,
For to spread abroad to King George's fleet
That we'll run the risk or else we'll die!'

The fight begun 'bout six in the morning,
And on to the setting of the sun.
Oh, and at the rising of the next morning,
Out of ten ships we couldn't see but one.

Oh, three we sank and three we burned,
And three we caused to run away,
And one we brought into Portsmouth harbour,
For to let them know we had won the day.

If anyone then should enquire
Or want to know our captain's name,
Oh, Captain Wellfounder's our chief commander,
But the *Royal Oak* is our ship by name.

THE SAILOR FROM DOVER

Sung by Mrs Lucy Durston, Bridgwater, Som. (C.J.S. 1909)

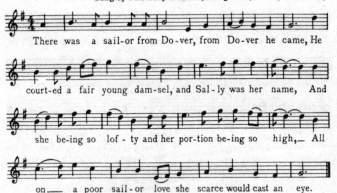

There was a sail-or from Do-ver, from Do-ver he came, He court-ed a fair young dam-sel, and Sal-ly was her name, And she be-ing so lof-ty and her por-tion be-ing so high,— All on— a poor sail-or love she scarce would cast an eye.

There was a sailor from Dover, from Dover he came,
He courted a fair young damsel, and Sally was her name,
And she being so lofty and her portion being so high,
All on a poor sailor love she scarce would cast an eye.

'O Sally, dearest Sally, O Sally,' then said he,
'I fear that your false heart my ruin it will be;
Without your present hatred is turnèd into love,
You'll make me broken-hearted and my ruin it will prove.'

'I cannot love a sailor, nor any such a man,
So keep your heart in comfort and forget me if you can.
I pray you keep your distance and mind your own discourse,
For I never intend to marry you unless that I am forced.'

But when a year was over and twelve months they was past,
This lovely young damsel she grew sick in love at last.
Entangled she was all in her love, she did not know for why,
So she sent for the young man on whom she had an eye.

'Oh, am I now the doctor, that you have sent for me?
Pray don't you well remember how once you slighted me?
How once you slighted me, my love, and treated me with scorn?
So now I will reward you for all that you have done.'

'For what is past and gone,' she said, 'I pray you to forgive,
And grant me just a little longer time for to live.'
'Oh no, my dearest Sally, as long as I have breath,
I'll dance all on your grave, love, as you lie under the earth.'

A SAILOR IN THE NORTH COUNTRY

Sung by Mrs Verrall, Horsham, Sussex (R.V.W. 1904)

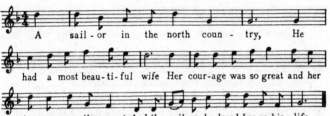

A sailor in the north country, He had a most beautiful wife Her courage was so great and her temper more than sweet, And the sailor he loved her as his life.

A sailor in the north country,
He had a most beautiful wife.
Her courage was so great and her temper
    more than sweet,
And the sailor he loved her as his life.

As they were walking out one day,
They met a noble captain on the way,
Kind obedience to the maid! But she
    bowed and nothing said,
'Twas her beauty did the captain's heart
    betray.

The captain to his house then he goes,
And sent for the sailor straight away,
'My business runs so: to the West Indies
    you must go,
In the morning, or by the break of day.'

'To obey the noble Master I will go,
On the sea, to venture my life.'
But little did he dream the captain's
    heart was so inflamed,
On the charms of his most beautiful wife.

The sailor to his wife then he goes,
And kissed her and called her his dear.
'Bad news I have to tell you, I must bid
    you farewell,
In the morning when daylight does
    appear.'

As soon as she heard him say so,
She wrung her hands and bitterly did cry,
She kissed him and said: 'My dear
    Jimmy I'm afraid
You'll be drowned in the raging ocean
    wide.'

The hour and the moment did come,
The poor sailor no longer could stay
To hear his wife lament till his heart
    was discontent.
He kissed her and went weeping away.

He had only been gone two days or three
On the seas for to venture his life,
Before the captain came with his heart
    in great flame,
To seize on the poor sailor's wife.

'Your pardon, dear lady,' he cried,
'Your pardon, dear lady, if you please,
Your pardon if you please, for 'tis you
    can give me ease
One night to enjoy your sweet charms.'

'Oh, are you any lord, duke, or king,
Or are you any ruler of the land?
The King shall lose his crown before
    at my feet you shall lie down,
Or before I will be at your command.

''Twas only one twelve-month ago
    That I was made your man Jimmy's bride,
    It's pleasing to my lot, the best husband I have got,
    I'll be constant unto him for life.'

A SAILOR'S LIFE

Sung by Henry Hills, Lodsworth, Sussex (W.P.M. 1899)

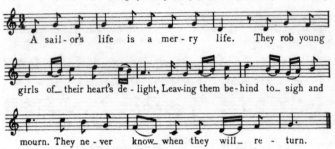

A sail-or's life is a mer-ry life. They rob young girls of_ their heart's de-light, Leav-ing them be-hind to_ sigh and mourn. They ne-ver know_ when they will_ re-turn.

A sailor's life is a merry life.
They rob young girls of their heart's delight,
Leaving them behind to sigh and mourn.
They never know when they will return.

Here's four and twenty all in a row.
My sweetheart cuts the brightest show;
He's proper, tall, genteel withal,
And if I don't have him I'll have none at all.

O father, fetch me a little boat,
That I might on the ocean float,
And every Queen's ship that we pass by,
We'll make enquire for my sailor boy.

We had not sailed long upon the deep,
Before a Queen's ship we chanced to meet.
'You sailors all, come tell me true,
Does my sweet William sail among your crew?'

'Oh no, fair lady, he is not here,
For he is drowned, we greatly fear.
On yon green island as we passed by,
There we lost sight of your sailor boy.'

She wrung her hands and she tore her hair,
Much like a woman in great despair.
Her little boat 'gainst a rock did run.
'How can I live now my William is gone?'

SALISBURY PLAIN

Sung by Mr and Mrs Verrall, Horsham, Sussex (R.V.W. 1904)

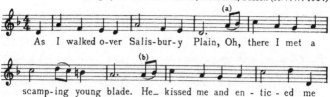

As I walked o-ver Salis-bur-y Plain, Oh, there I met a

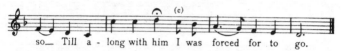

scamp-ing young blade. He_ kissed me and en - tic - ed me

so_ Till a - long with him I was forced for to go.

Some versions have (a) and (b) (c)

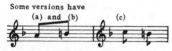

Verse 5 begins:

Ear - ly next morn- ing my love he a - rose, And so

nim - bly he put_ on his clothes.

As I walked over Salisbury Plain,
Oh, there I met a scamping young blade.
He kissed me and enticed me so
Till along with him I was forced for to go.

We came unto a public house at last,
And there for man and wife we did pass.
He called for ale and wine and strong
beer,
Till at length we both to bed did repair.

'Undress yourself, my darling,' says he.
'Undress yourself, and come to bed with
me.'
'Oh yes, that I will,' then says she,
'If you'll keep all those flash girls away.'

'Those flash girls you need not fear,
For you'll be safe-guarded, my dear.
I'll maintain you as some lady so gay,
For I'll go a-robbing on the highway.'

Early next morning my love he arose,
And so nimbly he put on his clothes.
Straight to the highway he set sail,
And 'twas there he robbed the coaches
of the mail.

Oh, it's now my love in Newgate Jail do
lie,
Expecting every moment to die.
The Lord have mercy on his poor soul,
For I think I hear the death-bell for to
toll.

THE SHIP IN DISTRESS

Sung by Mr Harwood, Watersfield, Sussex (G.B. 1907)

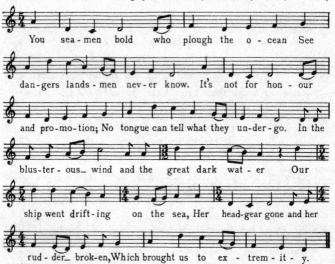

You seamen bold who plough the ocean See dangers landsmen never know. It's not for honour and promotion; No tongue can tell what they undergo. In the blusterous wind and the great dark water Our ship went drifting on the sea, Her head-gear gone and her rudder broken, Which brought us to extremity.

You seamen bold who plough the ocean
See dangers landsmen never know.
It's not for honour and promotion;
No tongue can tell what they undergo.
In the blusterous wind and the great dark
     water
Our ship went drifting on the sea,
Her headgear gone, and her rudder
     broken,
Which brought us to extremity.

For fourteen days, heartsore and hungry,
Seeing but wild water and bitter sky,
Poor fellows, they stood in a totter,
A-casting lots as to which should die.
The lot it fell on Robert Jackson,
Whose family was so very great.
'I'm free to die, but oh, my comrades,
Let me keep look-out till the break of
     day.'

A full-dressed ship like the sun a-glittering
Came bearing down to their relief.
As soon as this glad news was shouted,
It banished all their care and grief.
The ship brought to, no longer drifting,
Safe in Saint Vincent, Cape Verde, she gained.
You seamen all, who hear my story,
Pray you'll never suffer the like again.

SIX DUKES WENT A-FISHING

Sung by George Gouldthorpe, Brigg, Lincs. (P.G. 1906)

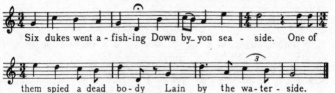

Six dukes went a-fish-ing Down by_ yon sea - side. One of
them spied a dead bo-dy Lain by the wa-ter-side.

Six dukes went a-fishing
Down by yon sea-side.
One of them spied a dead body
Lain by the waterside.

The one said to the other,
These words I heard them say:
'It's the Royal Duke of Grantham
That the tide has washed away.'

They took him up to Portsmouth,
To a place where he was known;
From there up to London,
To the place where he was born.

They took out his bowels,
And stretched out his feet,
And they balmed his body
With roses so sweet.

Six dukes stood before him,
Twelve raised him from the ground,
Nine lords followed after him
In their black mourning gown.

Black was their mourning,
And white were the wands,
And so yellow were the flamboys
That they carried in their hands.

He now lies betwixt two towers,
He now lies in cold clay,
And the Royal Queen of Grantham
Went weeping away.

Ralph Vaughan Williams and A. L. Lloyd

THE STREAMS OF LOVELY NANCY

Sung by George Dowden, Lackington, Dorset (H.E.D.H. 1905)

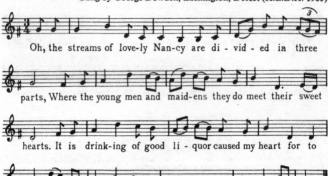

Oh, the streams of love-ly Nan-cy are di - vid - ed in three parts, Where the young men and maid-ens they do meet their sweet hearts. It is drink-ing of good li - quor caused my heart for to sing, And the noise in yon-der vil-lage made the rocks for to_ ring.

Oh, the streams of lovely Nancy are divided in three parts,
Where the young men and maidens they do meet their sweethearts.
It is drinking of good liquor caused my heart for to sing,
And the noise in yonder village made the rocks for to ring.

At the top of this mountain, there my love's castle stands.
Its all overbuilt with ivory on yonder black sand,
Fine arches, fine porches, and diamonds so bright.
It's a pilot for a sailor on a dark winter's night.

On yonder high mountain, where the wild fowl do fly,
There is one amongst them that flies very high.
If I had her in my arms, love, near the diamond's black land,
How soon I'd secure her by the sleight of my hand.

At the bottom of this mountain there runs a river clear.
A ship from the Indies did once anchor there,
With her red flags a-flying and the beating of her drum,
Sweet instruments of music and the firing of her gun.

So come all you little streamers that walk the meadows gay,
I'll write unto my own true love, wherever she may be.
For her rosy lips entice me, with her tongue she tells me 'No',
And an angel might direct us right, and where shall we go?

THE TREES THEY GROW SO HIGH

Sung by unnamed woman singer, Stoke Fleming, Devon (B.B. n.d.)

The trees they grow so high and the leaves they grow so

green. The day is past and gone, my love, that you and I— have

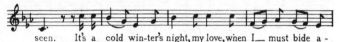

seen. It's a cold win-ter's night, my love, when I— must bide a-

-lone, For my bon-ny lad is young but a-grow-ing.—

The trees they grow so high and the leaves they grow so green.
The day is past and gone, my love, that you and I have seen.
It's a cold winter's night, my love, when I must bide alone,
For my bonny lad is young but a-growing.

As I was a-walking by yonder church wall,
I saw four and twenty young men a-playing at the ball.
I asked for my own true love but they would not let him come,
For they said the boy was young, but a-growing.

'O father, dearest father, you've done to me much wrong.
You've tied me to a boy when you know he is too young.'
'O daughter, dearest daughter, if you'll wait a little while,
A lady you shall be, while he's growing.

'We'll send your love to college, all for a year or two,
And then perhaps in time the boy will do for you.
I'll buy you white ribbons to tie about his waist,
To let the ladies know that he's married.'

And so early in the morning at the dawning of the day,
They went out into the hayfield to have some sport and play,
And what they did there, she never would declare,
But she never more complained of his growing.

And at the age of sixteen he was a married man,
And at the age of seventeen she brought to him a son,
And at the age of eighteen the grass grew over him,
And that soon put an end to his growing.

Ralph Vaughan Williams and A. L. Lloyd

THE WHALE-CATCHERS

Sung by Henry Hills, Lodsworth, Sussex (W.P.M. 1900)

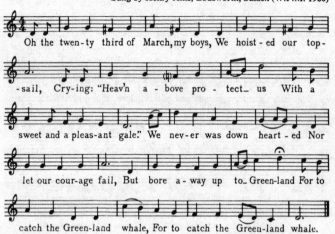

Oh the twen-ty third of March, my boys, We hoist-ed our top-sail, Cry-ing: "Heav'n a-bove pro-tect_ us With a sweet and a pleas-ant gale." We nev-er was down heart-ed Nor let our cour-age fail, But bore a-way up to_ Green-land For to catch the Green-land whale, For to catch the Green-land whale.

On the twenty-third of March, my boys,
We hoisted our topsail,
Crying: 'Heav'n above protect us
With a sweet and a pleasant gale.'
We never was down-hearted
Nor let our courage fail,
But bore away up to Greenland
For to catch the Greenland whale,
For to catch the Greenland whale.

And when we came to Greenland
Where the bitter winds did blow,
We tacked about all in the north
Among the frost and snow.
Our finger-tops were frozen off,
And likewise our toe-nails,
As we crawled on the deck, my boys,
Looking out for the Greenland whale
Looking out for the Greenland whale.

And when we came to Imez,
Where the mountains flowed with snow,
We tacked about all in the north
Till we heard a whalefish blow.
And when we catch this whale, brave boys,
Homeward we will steer.
We'll make the valleys ring, my boys,
A-drinking of strong beer.
We'll make those lofty alehouses
In London town to roar;
And when our money is all gone,
To Greenland go for more,
To Greenland go for more.

WHEN I WAS A LITTLE BOY

Sung by John Stickle, Baltasound, Unst, Shetland (P.S.-S. 1947)

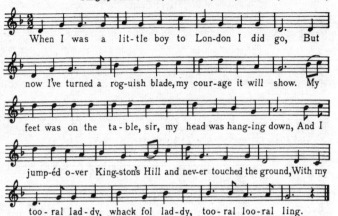

When I was a little boy to London I did go,
But now I've turned a roguish blade, my courage it will show.
My feet was on the table, sir, my head was hanging down,
And I jumpéd over Kingston's Hill and never touched the ground,
    With my tooral laddy, whack fol laddy, tooral looral ling.

I bought myself a little bull about three inches high;
The people all admired me, it's for to hear him cry.
The people all admired me for he made such an awful sound,
He made the steeple of St Paul's Church come tumbling to the ground
    With my, etc.

I bought myself a flock of sheep and most of them were wethers;
Sometimes they brought me fine wool, sometimes they brought me feathers.
They were as fine a flock, sir, as anyone could possess,
For every month or six weeks' time they brought me six lambs apiece,
    With my, etc.

I bought myself a little hen, and of her I took great care;
I set her on a mussel shell and she hatched me out a hare.
The hare grew up a milk-white steed about eighteen yards high,
And if anyone tell you a bigger story, I'll tell you it's a bloody lie.
    With my, etc.

I bought myself a little box about three acres square;
I stowed it into my breeches pocket, the guineas they were there.
Now the people all admired me, thanked me for what I'd done,
And they gave me a portion of silver and gold about ten thousand ton,
    With my, etc.

Ralph Vaughan Williams and A. L. Lloyd

WHEN I WAS YOUNG

Sung by Mrs Moore, High Heworth, Co. Durham (W.G.W. 1920)

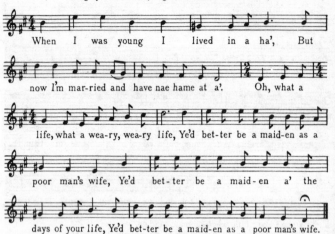

When I was young I lived in a ha',
But now I'm married and have nae hame at a'.
  Oh, what a life, what a weary, weary life,
  Ye'd better be a maiden as a poor man's wife,
  Ye'd better be a maiden a' the days of your life,
  Ye'd better be a maiden as a poor man's wife.

When I was young I used to sport and play,
But now I'm married and the cradle's in the way.
  Oh, what a life, etc.

When I was young I wore my slippers thin,
But now I'm married and the water it runs in.
  Oh, what a life, etc.

YE MAR'NERS ALL

Sung by Mrs Russell, Upwey, Dorset (H.E.D.H. 1907)

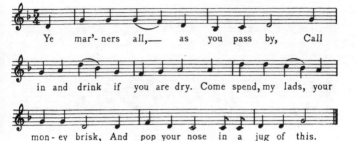

Ye mar'-ners all,— as you pass by, Call
in and drink if you are dry. Come spend, my lads, your
mon-ey brisk, And pop your nose in a jug of this.

Ye mar'ners all, as you pass by,
Call in and drink if you are dry.
Come spend, my lads, your money brisk,
And pop your nose in a jug of this.

Oh, mar'ners all, if you've half a crown,
You're welcome all for to sit down.
Come spend, my lads, your money brisk,
And pop your nose in a jug of this.

Oh, tipplers all, as ye pass by,
Come in and drink if you are dry.
Call in and drink, think not amiss,
And pop your nose in a jug of this.

Oh, now I'm old and can scarcely crawl,
I've an old grey beard and a head that's bald,
Crown my desire and fulfil my bliss,
A pretty girl and a jug of this.

Oh, when I'm in my grave and dead,
And all my sorrows are past and fled,
Transform me then into a fish,
And let me swim in a jug of this.

THE YOUNG AND SINGLE SAILOR

Sung by Mr Burridge, near Capel, Surrey (R.V.W. 1908)

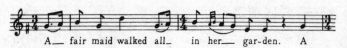

A— fair maid walked all— in her— gar-den. A

brisk young sail-or she chanced to spy. He— stepped up to her, think-

-ing to view her. Says he: 'Fair maid, could you fan-cy me?'

A fair maid walked all in her garden.
A brisk young sailor she chanced to spy.
He stepped up to her, thinking to view her.
Says he: 'Fair maid, could you fancy me?'

'Oh no, young man, you're a man of honour,
A man of honour you seem to be.
So don't impose on a poor young woman
Who is scarce fitted your servant to be.'

'If you tell me you're a poor young woman,
The more regard I shall have for you.
So come with me and I'll make you happy,
And you'll have servants for to wait on you.'

'Oh no, young man, I have a sweetheart,
And seven long years he's away from me,
And seven more I will wait for him,
And if he's alive he will return to me.'

'Oh, seven years makes an alteration.
Perhaps he's drowned and is now at rest.'
'Then no other man shall ever join me,
For he's the darling boy that I love best.'

He put his hand all in his pocket,
His fingers being both long and small,
Saying: 'Here's the ring, love, we broke between us.'
Soon as she saw it, then she down did fall.

He took her close all in his arrums,
He gave her kisses by one, two, three,
Saying: 'I'm your young and single sailor,
That has come home for to marry thee.'

Ralph Vaughan Williams and A. L. Lloyd

YOUNG EDWIN IN THE LOWLANDS LOW

Sung by Mrs Hopkins, Axford, Basingstoke, Hants. (C.G. and R.V.W. 1907)

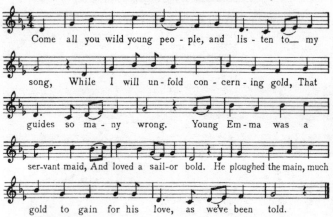

Come all you wild young peo - ple, and lis - ten to my song, While I will un - fold con - cern - ing gold, That guides so ma - ny wrong. Young Em - ma was a ser-vant maid, And loved a sail-or bold. He ploughed the main, much gold to gain for his love, as we've been told.

Come all you wild young people, and listen to my song,
While I will unfold concerning gold, that guides so many wrong.
Young Emma was a servant maid and loved a sailor bold.
He ploughed the main, much gold to gain for his love, as we've been told.

He ploughed the main for seven years and then he returned home.
As soon as he set foot on shore, unto his love did go.
He went unto young Emma's house, his gold all for to show,
That he had gained upon the main, all in the Lowlands low.

'My father keeps a public house down by the side of the sea,
And you go there and stay the night, and there you wait for me.
I'll meet you in the morning, but don't let my parents know
Your name it is Young Edwin that ploughed the Lowlands low.'

Young Edwin he sat drinking till time to go to bed.
He little thought a sword that night would part his body and head,
And Edwin he got into bed and scarcely was asleep,
When Emily's cruel parents soft into his room did creep.

They stabbed him, dragged him out of bed, and to the sea did go.
They sent his body floating down to the Lowlands low.
As Emily she lay sleeping, she had a dreadful dream;
She dreamed she saw Young Edwin's blood a-flowing like the stream.

'Oh father, where's the stranger come here last night to lay?'
'Oh, he is dead, no tales can tell,' her father he did say.
'Then father, cruel father, you'll die a public show,
For the murdering of Young Edwin that ploughed the Lowlands low.

'The fishes of the ocean swim o'er my lover's breast.
His body rolls in motion, I hope his soul's at rest.
The shells along the seashore that are rolling to and fro
Remind me of my Edwin that ploughed the Lowlands low.'

So many a day she passed away and tried to ease her mind,
And Emma, broken-hearted, was to Bedlam forced to go.
Crying: 'Oh, my friends, my love is gone, and I am left behind.'
Her shrieks were for Young Edwin that ploughed the Lowlands low.

Ralph Vaughan Williams and A. L. Lloyd

THE YOUNG GIRL CUT DOWN IN HER PRIME

Sung by an unnamed singer, East Meon, Hants (F.J. 1909)

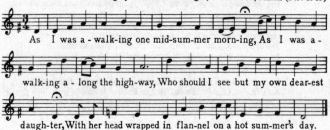

As I was a-walking one midsummer morning, As I was a-walking a-long the high-way, Who should I see but my own dear-est daugh-ter, With her head wrapped in flan-nel on a hot sum-mer's day.

As I was a-walking one midsummer morning,
As I was a-walking along the highway,
Who should I see but my own dearest daughter,
With her head wrapped in flannel on a hot summer's day.

'O mother, dear mother, come set you down by me.
Come set you down by me and pity my case;
For my wounds are now aching, my poor heart is breaking,
And I'm in low spirits and surely must die.

'O mother, dear mother, come send for the clergyman,
O send for the doctor to bind up my wound,
And likewise my young man, whose heart it did wander,
That he may see me before I'm screwed down.

'And when I am dead to the churchyard they'll bear me,
Six jolly fellows to carry me on,
And in each of their hands a bunch of green laurel,
So they may not smell me as they're walking along.

'So rattle your drums and play your fife over me,
So rattle your drums as we march along.
Then return to your home and think on that young girl:
"Oh, there goes a young girl cut down in her prime."'

LIST OF COLLECTORS

A.G.G.	Anne G. Gilchrist	F.J.	Francis Jekyll	P.G.	Percy Grainger
B.B.	Bertha Bidder	G.B.	George Butterworth	P.S.S.	Patrick
C.C.	Clive Carey	G.B.G.	George B. Gardiner		Shuldham-Shaw
C.G.	Charles Gamblin	G.E.McC.	G. E. McCleay	R.V.W.	R. Vaughan Williams
C.J.S.	Cecil J. Sharp	H.E.D.H.	H. E. D. Hammond	T.A.	Tilly Aston
E.B.	Ella Bell	J.E.T.	J. E. Thomas	W.F.	Walter Ford
E.J.M.	E. J. Moeran	L.E.B.	Lucy E. Broadwood	W.G.W.	W. G. Whittaker
E.M.L.	Ella M. Leather	M.E.S.	Mary E. Spence	W.P.M.	W. Percy Merrick
E.T.S.	E. T. Sweeting	M.S.	Marie Slocombe		

Notes on the Songs

Abbreviations

(For the convenience of readers who may already be accustomed to using the invaluable *Guide to English Folk Song Collections* by Margaret Dean-Smith, we have generally adopted the letter-signs used in that work.)

BCS   Broadwood, L. E., *English County Songs*. London, 1893.
BF   Barrett, W. A., *English Folk Songs*. London, 1891.
BGG   Baring Gould, S., and others, *A Garland of Country Song*. London, 1895.
BGS   Baring Gould, S., and Sharp, C. J., *English Folk Songs for Schools*. London, 1906.
BGSW Baring Gould, S., and others, *Songs of the West* (revised ed.). London, 1905.
BSFL Burne, C., *Shropshire Folk-lore*. London, 1883.
BTSC Broadwood, L. E., *English Traditional Songs and Carols*. London, 1908.
FSJ   *Journal of the Folk Song Society*. London, 1899–1931.
GFH   Gardiner, G. B., *Folk Songs from Hampshire*. London, 1909.
GOR   Gillington, A. E., *Songs of the Open Road*. London, 1911.
JEFDSS *Journal of the English Folk Dance and Song Society* (successor to FSJ). London, 1931–.
KG   Kidson, F., *A Garland of English Folk Songs*. London, 1926.
KPS   Kidson, F., *English Peasant Songs*. London, 1929.

KTT   Kidson, F., *Traditional Tunes*. Oxford, 1891.

MSS   Moeran, E. J., *Six Suffolk Folk Songs*. London, 1932.

SEF(I–II)   Sharp, C. J., *English Folk Songs*. London, 1921.

SFS(I–V)   Sharp, C. J., and (for Series I–III) Marson, C. L., *Folk Songs from Somerset*. London, 1904–9.

WSS   Whall, W. B., *Sea Songs and Shanties* (revised ed.). Glasgow, 1920.

WUT   Williams, A., *Folk Songs of the Upper Thames*. London, 1923.

All Things are Quite Silent (FSJ II 202)

Even in Nelson's day, when the sailor with his tarry pigtail was the nation's pride, so notorious were conditions aboard the royal ships that the Navy could only be maintained by pressing men to sea. The press-gangs were the terror to life along the coasts of England, tearing men from the seamen's tavern or the plough, or even (some songs tell us) from the marriage bed, to serve in the warships with no prospect of release till the end of the war, whenever that might be. Here is one among many lamentations of wives bereft of their husbands by the press-gang. The song presumably belongs to a period before 1835, for by that time the system of impressment had almost faded out, though it was never actually abolished by Act of Parliament. This seems to be the only version of the song reported from oral tradition.

As Sylvie Was Walking (JEFDSS 152)

This song was sent to W. P. Merrick from Australia. The singer, an eighty-year-old woman born near Coleford, Glos., had been living in the Antipodes since 1855. She learned the song from her uncle, also from Gloucestershire. The text has been amplified from versions sung to H. E. D. Hammond in 1906 by two Dorset women, Mrs Hann of Stoke Abbot and Mrs Russell of Upwey. A version from Lew Down, Devon, appears in BGSW 78–9 under the title of *A Maiden Sat a-Weeping*.

The Banks of Green Willow (FSJ II 34)

There is a common superstition, older than Jonah, that the presence of a wrongdoer aboard ship may make the vessel unmanageable. Disaster may result unless the offender is discovered and thrown overboard. A Scottish text printed in 1827 makes it clear that the 'Jonah' motive lies within this song, though the twentieth-century versions are so disordered that the meaning is rather obscured. The full story concerns a young woman who robs her parents, at her lover's request, and sails away with him. During a storm at sea the woman gives birth to a baby. The sailors fear that someone aboard is flying from retribution. The blame is fixed on the woman, and to her lover's grief she is thrown overboard. Later versions, however, make it seem that the lover is the murderer. Fifty years ago Sharp reported the song 'very generally sung throughout Somerset'. Five of Sharp's nine Somerset versions are given in FSJ II 33–6, and FSJ III 292 has a Hampshire version noted by R. Vaughan Williams.

The Banks of Newfoundland (FSJ VIII 99)

Cecil Sharp collected a version of this song from a seaman aboard the American liner S.S. *St Paul*, in 1915 (FSJ V 300–1). Sharp describes it as a capstan shanty, but its use as such must have been very limited. The song seems to have been very more commonly used as a forebitter or foc'sle song, sung for diversion. In both text and melody, there are remarkable similarities to some sets of the (slightly earlier) transportation ballad, *Van Diemen's Land*. The incident of the dream, the names of the crew members, the detail of the good-hearted lady passenger, are all borrowed from the older ballad. Mr Farr, who was seventy-six when this song was noted from him, had a fine repertory of shanties. His text of *The Banks of Newfoundland* was almost identical with that of Sharp's informant, but we have borrowed a few phrases from the latter, also the device of the 'holy-stoning' chorus, which, in Mr Farr's version, occurred only at the end of the song. The tune is related to some Irish sets of *The Lowlands of Holland*.

The Banks of Sweet Primroses (FSJ IV 1124)

We have included this well-favoured piece as representative of a large and important class of English folk songs. Sharp found it several times in Devon and Somerset, and he includes a version from Mrs Lucy White of Hambridge in SFS I 8. In a note he mentions that the words are to be found 'on broadsides by Barraclough of Nuneaton and others'. The complete song was first printed in 1891 (BF 80). There is a North Country version in KG 56, and South Country ones in Gillington's *Eight Hampshire Folk Songs* (1907) and Carey's *Ten English Folk Songs* (1915). FSJ I 121 has a Sussex set from Mr Copper of Rottingdean. Versions from Devon, Kent, and Essex (four examples) are in FSJ IV 124–6. In JEFDSS VII 151 is a version recorded in 1952 in the 'home-made' harmonies of the Copper family. In the 1930s, Philip Tanner of Gower, South Wales, recorded the song on a commercial gramophone record (Columbia FB 1570, later re-issued as RO 101). Tune and text have shown remarkable constancy through these several versions. Clearly, singers have found the song unusually

memorable and satisfactory, for the process of oral transmission seems to have worked little change on it.

The Basket of Eggs (FSJ II 102)

This wry song of two sailors who thought to outwit a trusting
girl and were themselves tricked, has been found in slightly
differing versions in districts as far apart as Norfolk (FSJ I 46
and II 103) and Herefordshire (FSJ II 102), Sussex (FSJ II 102)
and Shetland (JEFDSS VI 16). It is sometimes confused with *The
Oyster Girl*, a song that gained wide currency in the nineteenth
century through its use by popular stage comedians.
However, the two songs seem to be separate.

Benjamin Bowmaneer (JEFDSS I 97)

In folklore, the poor tailor seldom plays a noble part, perhaps
because his profession does not call for lustihood 'Nine
tailors make a man' says the proverb, and a popular children's
rhyme tells of four and twenty tailors frightened by a snail.
The amusing *Benjamin Bowmaneer* seems to perpetuate the
folks' injustice to men of an honorable trade. Perhaps the
song has a secondary, satirical meaning that eludes us? It has
been suggested that 'Castors away' may mean 'Hats off',
the castors being a slang word for a beaver hat, or by exten-
sion, any headgear. It may also mean 'Cast us away!', and thus
be related to a sailors' song. The tune's resemblance to the
Spanish Ladies melody, much used for sea-song texts would
seem to strengthen this possibility. We have not found a set of
this song complete with tune elsewhere.

The Blacksmith (FSJ VIII 208)

The faithful 'hero' of this song is just as often a shoemaker as a blacksmith. Both metre and tune are rather unusual, recalling the well-known *Brisk Young Widow* in SFS III, and *Brave Wolfe*, a song celebrating the hero of Quebec, often found in America though not reported in Britain (*Brave Wolfe* is not to be confused with *Bold General Wolfe*, which is fairly common in England). The opening of the 'strange news' verse also appears in some sets of *Brave Wolfe*. *The Blacksmith* (or *Shoemaker*) has been reported from Sussex (FSJ IV 279), Essex (FSJ IV 280), Herefordshire (FSJ IV 280 – two versions), Somerset (FSJ VIII 17), and Dorset (FSJ VIII 206).

The Bold Benjamin (FSJ III 93)

The singer learned this song from a man-o'-war's man in the 1850s. We know no details of the unlucky expedition it celebrates. The song is a latter-day re-make of a black-letter ballad, published *c.* 1670, called *The Benjamin's Lamentation for their Sad Loss at Sea, etc.* (Roxburghe Ballads, VII 529), beginning 'Captain Chilver's gone to sea, I, boys, O boys!'. C. H. Firth, in *Naval Songs and Ballads* (Navy Records Society, 1908), remarks on the interesting metrical form of *The Benjamin's Lamentation*, and suggests that it may be an early shanty.

The Bramble Briar (FSJ V 123)

This interesting ballad, not included in the Child compilation, is based on a story that was probably not new when Boccaccio made it famous in the fourteenth century. Hans Sachs put it into verse some two hundred years later, and in the nineteenth century, Keats re-wrote it as *Isabella and the Pot of Basil*.

The English traditional versions are quite unlike Keats's, but are very close to Hans Sachs's rendering. Besides this Hertfordshire version, sets of the ballad have been reported in print from Somerset (FSJ II 42, V 126) and Hampshire (GOR p. 10). Mrs Joiner was unable to remember clearly the beginning of the ballad, and our first two stanzas are from the version obtained by Cecil Sharp from Mrs Overd of Langport, Somerset, in 1904.

The Broomfield Hill (FSJ IV 114)

This ancient ballad was a great favourite with singers in England and Scotland. Sharp alone collected at least twelve distinct versions. It was often printed on broadsheets and in America a good version found its way into a popular pocket song book, *The Pearl Songster*, about the middle of the nineteenth century. Some texts make it clear that the bold girl had bewitched the lover into his deep sleep. In England, other versions of the song have been reported from Dorset (FSJ III 69, IV 115, VII 31), Lincs. (FSJ IV 110), Somerset (FSJ IV 112, VII 33), Norfolk, Hereford (both FSJ IV 114), and Essex (FSJ VIII 127).

The Cock-Fight (*The Bonny Grey*) (FSJ II 84)

It is generally agreed that the weight and blackness of the Industrial Revolution took the heart out of most of our folk-singers. Yet some fine songs lingered on in industrial towns, and balladeers who made songs for Lancashire spinners and Yorkshire weavers and Cumberland and Durham miners were still at work late in the nineteenth century. They no longer sang of the clash of bright swords. Rather they preferred to take the popular newspaper themes – murder, adultery, prize-fighting, sometimes horse-racing. Long after cockfighting was made illegal, the cruel sport and its lively ballad persisted on the northern moors and fells. Various versions place the cockfight at Walney Island in Westmorland, at Holbeck Moor and Hunslet in Yorkshire, and in Liverpool. All agree that after a hard fight the Bonny Grey was the victor.

The text, sung to Cecil Sharp by Mr Collinson at the Kendal folk song competition in 1905, is amended and clarified from a Yorkshire version in KTT, a Lancashire version in A. L. Lloyd's *Come All ye Bold Miners*, and from the broadsheet printed by Harkness of Preston.

The Cruel Mother (FSJ III 71)

The great Scottish collector Gavin Greig believed that 'the numerous versions of this ballad are practically all Scottish', but in fact it has been widespread in England too, a form of it even turning up as a London children's street game (N. Douglas, *London Street Games*, 1931 ed., p. 47). Apart from that version, and our Essex set, the ballad has been reported from oral tradition in Oxfordshire (FSUT p. 295), Shropshire (SFL p. 540), Dorset (FSJ III 70, 71), Somerset (SFS IV 54), and (again as a game song) in Lancashire (FSJ VI 80).

The Daughter of Peggy, O (FSJ V 260)

The cautionary tale of the shrew tamed by flogging seems to have been common in bygone days, first as a serious homily, later as comedy. It has given rise to many songs, including *The Wife Wrapt in Wether's Skin* (Child 277), the well-known *Wee Cooper o' Fife*, *Ruggleton's Daughter of Iero* (SFS IV 52), the nursery ballad *Robin-a-Thrush* (BGS 102), and *On Monday Morning* (p. 76 in this present collection).

Death and the Lady (FSJ V 19)

In the Middle Ages, the Dance of Death and dialogues between Death and his victim used to be enacted as a stage morality. Later, the theme was taken up by artists as great as Holbein and as humble as the chapbook illustrators. Miss Anne Gilchrist has noted (JEFDSS IV, 37–48) that 'in English balladry the favourite aspect of the subject was Death in its relation to radiant beauty and lusty and careless youth'. The ballad, perhaps of late sixteenth-century origin, was originally in dialogue-form and it may well have been at once sung and acted. Traditional versions have also been noted from Devon (BGSW 202–3), Somerset (SFS IV 4), Wiltshire (WUT 173), and Sussex (BTSC 40).

The Death of Queen Jane (FSJ III 67)

The story is a legendary re-working of historical fact. Jane Seymour, wife of Henry VIII, died on 24 October 1537, twelve days after the natural birth of her son, who later became Edward VI. Some said her death was due to clumsy surgery. We do not know how old this ballad is, nor if it derives from a piece called *The Lamentation of Queen Jane*, licensed for publication in 1560. The ballad has been collected in Devon (FSJ II 222) and Somerset (FSJ V 257), and a second Dorset version is given in FSJ III 67. *The Death of Queen Jane* is No. 170 in Child's collection.

The Deserter from Kent (FSJ V 154)

Most of the songs about army deserters current in England have the ring of street balladry rather than of country tradition. Many appear to have been made by Irishmen. The present song would seem to be an exception. Two missing lines in the penultimate verse have been restored from the related Army song: *The Rambling Royal*. The text of *The Deserter from Kent* is rare, and only this version has appeared in print. The tune, however, is a variant of the familiar 'Villikins' air, perhaps the commonest of all British folk-melodies.

The Devil and the Ploughman (FSJ II 184)

The Devil comes to fetch a farmer's wife. The farmer is delighted. But the shrewish woman behaves so abominably in Hell that the Devil is obliged to bring her back again. The song, apparently common all over the British Isles and frequently recorded in America, seems to embody a very old joke indeed. Perhaps in early forms, the farmer had enlisted the Devil's aid with his ploughing, promising the soul of one of his family in return. Most versions of this song have a whistled refrain, and this is not without sly meaning, for there is an old belief that whistling summons the Devil (hence the sailors' superstition that whistling aboard ship may bring on a storm). Burns re-made a Scottish version of the ballad, and called it *The Carle o' Killyburn Braes*. Mrs Burns, speaking to a scholar of the way in which her husband altered folk songs, remarked: 'Robert gae this ane a terrible brushing.' Our text is filled out with some verses obtained by Alfred Williams from David Sawyer, of Ogbourne, Wilts. (WUT 211). A Dorset version is given in FSJ III 131–2.

Droylsden Wakes (FSJ V 204)

This Lancashire dialogue song was once associated with a folk ceremonial attached to the local 'wakes' or annual holiday. The custom was for two men in comic dress, one of them travestied as a woman, to sit in a cart with a spinning-wheel before them, spinning flax as they sang the song, and collecting money from onlookers. The ceremonial may go back to ancient times, though it does not seem to have reached Droylsden until early in the nineteenth century. The tune is of the primitive sort often used for wassails, May Day songs and other festive ceremonial purposes. There is some doubt whether the refrain means 'Tread the wheel' or 'Thread ye well'. A description of the ceremonial, with a text of the song, is in John Harland's *Ballads and Songs of Lancashire* (1865).

The False Bride (FSJ II 14)

This tender melancholy song has remained long in the affection of country singers. Its age is uncertain. A version of the ballad was published in Newcastle late in the seventeenth century, but it may not have been new then. It is still to be found among folk singers in the South of England. Some call it *The Week before Easter*, and sing the first verse:

> The week before Easter, the morn bright and clear,
> The sun it shone brightly and keen blowed the air,
> I went up in the forest for to gather fine flowers,
> But the forest won't yield me no roses.

Mrs White's text has been slightly amended with lines from two other Somerset versions collected by Sharp in 1904 (FSJ 12–13). Other versions have have been printed from Devon (BGSW 198) and Sussex (FSJ I 23).

The Gaol Song (FSJ VII 47)

English tradition includes many crime songs but relatively few dealing with life in prison. The broadside ballads of Bellevue, Wakefield, and Kirkdale gaols, published by Bebbington of Manchester and Harkness of Preston, all derive from the same 'original', issued several times in London by the Catnach Press and its successors as *The County Gaol*. A different ballad, called *Durham Gaol*, said to be the work of the pitman-balladeer Thomas Armstrong, was current on Tyneside till recently (see A. L. Lloyd, *Come All ye Bold Miners*). Each of these bears some relation to our *Gaol Song*, of which two versions, with separate melodies, were collected by H. E. D. Hammond in Beaminster, Dorset, in June 1906.

The Gentleman Soldier (FSJ V 156)

This jaunty song, common in the army and quoted by Kipling in *Soldiers Three*, has rarely found its way into the conventional song collections. The text, printed in incomplete form in the *Folk Song Journal*, is amplified from a Somerset version collected by H. E. D. Hammond and not hitherto published. The melody is a military-sounding version of the widespread tune called *Drumdelgie* in Scotland and *Dydd Llun y Boreu* in Wales.

Geordie (FSJ IV 333)

This ballad, No. 209 in Child, is well known both in England and Scotland. The Scottish sets differ considerably from the English ones, for in them the hero is not a thief but a nobleman, thought by some scholars to be George Gordon, Earl of Huntly, who suffered royal displeasure when he showed clemency towards a Highland robber in 1554. In the English versions, which may be re-makes of the Scottish, the main character is always an outlaw. An old black-letter ballad names him as George Stoole of Northumberland, who was executed in 1610; but even in its 'robber' form (if that is the more recent) the song probably pre-dates the seventeenth century. Mr Neville's tune is related to the well-known air of *Searching for Lambs*. *Geordie* has been found in oral tradition also in Sussex (FSJ I 164 and II 208), Cambridgeshire (FSJ II 47–9), Somerset (FSJ II 27–8 and IV 333), Norfolk (FSJ IV 89–90), Suffolk, Surrey and Dorset (FSJ IV 332–3), and Yorkshire (KT 24–6).

George Collins (FSJ III 301)

A man meets a girl by a stream; he kisses her; he returns home and dies; at the sight of his coffin, his true-love realizes the tragedy and prepares to die in turn. The plot of *George Collins* has its secrets. From an examination of a number of variants, the full story becomes clearer. The girl by the stream is a water-fairy. The young man has been in the habit of visiting her. He is about to marry a mortal, and the fairy takes her revenge with a poisoned kiss. The song telling that story is among the great ballads of Europe. Its roots and branches are spread in Scandinavia, Germany, France, Italy, Spain, and elsewhere. An early literary form is the German poem of the Knight of Staufenberg (*c.* 1310). France alone has about ninety versions, mostly in the form of the familiar *Renaud*, though here much of the dream-quality of the tale is missing, since the girl by the stream is lost sight of, and instead the hero is mortally wounded in battle. The first half of the *George Collins* story is told in the ballad called *Clerk Colvill* (Child 42), the second half in *Lady Alice* (Child 85). Either these are two separate songs which have been combined to form *George*

Collins or (which seems more likely) they are two fragments of the completed ballad. *George Collins* has rarely been reported in England, though in the summer of 1906 Dr G. B. Gardiner collected three separate versions in different Hampshire villages (two of them on the same day) (FSJ III 299–301).

The Golden Vanity (FSJ II 244)

In some versions of this favourite ballad, the enemy is Turkish; in others, he is Spanish or French. Rarely, the song has a happy ending, with the brave boy saved and rewarded. Occasionally it concludes with the boy drowned, and his ghost returning to sink his own ship. More usually it ends as here, with the boy rejected by the cruel captain and pulled aboard too late by his shipmates. Samuel Pepys preserved a seventeenth-century broadside version in which the hero was Sir Walter Raleigh, but later singers seem to have cast aside this detail. The melody given here is quite different from that usually taught in schools. The text comes in the main from the version collected in 1900 by W. P. Merrick from Henry Hills, of Shepperton, Sussex (FSJ I 104–5). Mr Bolton explained that the 'black bear-skin' was the cabin boy's covering at night, and that he wished to wear it as a disguise in the water. Other versions have been reported from Wiltshire (WUT 199–200) and Cornwall (BGSW 136–7).

The Green Bed (FSJ III 282)

During the nineteenth century the ballad press issued a large number of broadsides setting out the sailor's disgust with the treatment received at the hands of grasping landladies and their faithless daughters. That many of these songs resemble each other seems to be the result of influence rather than accident. *Green Beds*, 'a song popular both in the foc'sle and in the cottage', tells the tale in fullest detail and must be regarded as the most important ballad on this theme. A fairly close relative is the well-known song, *The Wild Rover*. *The Green Bed* has also been collected in Warwickshire (FSJ I 48), Somerset (FSJ V 68), and Devon (BGSW 186–7, with words re-written).

The Greenland Whale Fishery (FSJ II 243)

Until 1830, the whaling ships put out each spring from London, King's Lynn, Hull, Whitby, bound for the right-whale grounds of Greenland. The best of our whaling ballads are about the Greenland fishery. After 1830, the fleets moved to Baffin Bay, and subsequently to the grounds off Hawaii and Peru, but still most of the songs the whalermen sang were of the Greenland days. The present song is quite old, a form of it being published as a black-letter ballad before 1725. It was evidently popular in the nineteenth century, since Pitts, Such, and Catnach each issued broadside versions, giving 1824 as the date of the incident described. Sharp published a version in which the date is 1861 – thirty years too late for Greenland whaling. This adventurous song is still to be met with among traditional singers. This text comes partly from the broadsides by Catnach and Such. The song is also reported from Somerset (SFS III 54) and Norfolk (FSJ VIII 279), while Baring Gould (BGG 26) and Whall (WSS 69) have unlocated versions giving the date as 1794. The singer consistently sang an F sharp in the concluding phrase, though the tune has a strongly mixolydian character.

The Grey Cock or The Lover's Ghost (JEFDSS VII 97)

A number of lyrical folk songs present the situation of two lovers disturbed by the early crowing of a cock. Perhaps the origin of these songs is found in this supernatural ballad of the lover returned from the dead. The idea that such revenants must go again 'from the world of pity to the world without pity' when the birds cry at dawn is an ancient folklore notion that has spread from the Orient, through the Balkans, as far west as Ireland. Perhaps it is surprising to find such a rare ballad surviving as late as 1951 in the city of Birmingham, where it was recorded from an English-born singer of Irish descent. *The Grey Cock* appears as No. 248 in Child's collection, but not in such good shape as here.

I Wish, I Wish (JEFDSS VII 103)

Most English songs tell a story. However, there are also songs that are merely lyrical expressions of a mood – usually arising from love denied or betrayed. Such songs are not held together by any narrative; instead they employ a number of images and symbols that are combined and recombined in song after song. Thus whole songs may be made up from 'floating' verses familiar in other contexts, or attached to other melodies. The verses of *I Wish, I Wish* are most commonly found either in the song called *Waly Waly* or in *Died for Love*. Jazz enthusiasts may be interested in the apron-low, apron-high motive, which re-appears in the Blues called *Careless Love*. It was also used by John Clare in *A Faithless Shepherd*, a poem largely made up of traditional 'floaters'.

Jack the Jolly Tar (FSJ II 39)

Seafarers know this song better under the title of *Do me Ama*. Part of its appeal comes from the fact that the common sailor gets the better of the squire in such an audacious fashion. Here Jack is akin to some of the prankish heroes of the *Arabian Nights*, of Chaucer and Boccaccio. Mrs Hooper knew only one verse of the song. Our text is supplied from versions in common oral currency among seamen. Two other Somerset versions are given in FSJ II 38–9, and Whall (WSS 16) prints an unlocated set.

John Barleycorn (FSJ VIII 41)

This ballad is rather a mystery. Is it an unusually coherent folklore survival of the ancient myth of the slain and resurrected Corn-God, or is it the creation of an antiquarian revivalist, which has passed into popular currency and become 'folklorized'? It is in any case an old song, of which an elaborate form was printed in the reign of James I. It was widespread over the English and Scottish countryside, and Burns re-wrote a well-known version. During the present century, versions have been collected in Sussex (FSJ I 81), Hampshire (FSJ III 255 and 256), Surrey (FSJ VI 27–8), Somerset (SFS III 9 and IV 32), and Wiltshire (WUT 246). The tune is a variant of that usually associated with the carol, *Dives and Lazarus*.

Lisbon (FSJ II 22)

The theme of the Maiden Warrior, the girl who shows her courage on the field of battle, has held the interest of audiences since the days when the epic singers of ancient

Greece sang of Hippolyte and her Amazons. Usually, in the English ballads, the girls are impelled into battle by love, not by pugnacity. Devotion leads them to put on men's clothing and follow their serving sweethearts. The girls, though brave, are also mild, like our heroine, who is even prepared to step aside without complaint if her sweetheart finds another love while campaigning. The title of this ballad suggests that its setting is the Peninsular War of 1808, but the same story, with some identical verses, is told in the common ballad of *The Banks of the Nile*, referring to the expedition against the French in Egypt in 1801. The song is well known in Australia, but there the sailor (or soldier) has become a shearer who is obliged to leave his home for a distant shearing shed, and the girl's 'waist it is too slender and constitution too fine to eat the ram-stag mutton on the banks of the Condamine'. Traditional versions have also been reported from Sussex (FSJ II 191–2), Surrey (FSJ VI 17–18), and Dorset (FSJ VII 50–1).

Long Lankin (FSJ V 81)

In Scots versions of this bloody ballad (Child 93), the hero is a mason who builds a castle, is cheated of his payment, and makes a terrible retaliation. In the English versions this idea is lost, and Lambkin, Longkin, or Lankin is merely a lawless ruffian. Yet he is no ordinary robber, for it is not booty he is after, but revenge. Is he perhaps a runaway serf with a grudge against his master? Or is he, as has been suggested, a desperate leper seeking the old folk-cure of the blood of an innocent, caught in a silver bowl? It is hard to guess the age of this ballad. Bishop Percy printed a version from Kent in 1775, and in the following year Herd published a Scottish text. The two versions differ in several details, and it is likely that the ballad was already old then. The strongest Scots tradition names Balwearie Castle as the scene – and its building in 1464 as the occasion – of the crime. Tradition is not evidence, but the song is probably based on a real event.

'Blood-boltered' as it is, *Lankin* retained a strong grip on the imagination of many singers, including the nun who sang the present version to Cecil Sharp. Further versions will be found in FSJ from Surrey (I 212–13), and Hampshire (II 111–12). The ballad is studied in JEFDSS I 1–7.

Lord Thomas and Fair Eleanor (FSJ II 107)

The theme of this ballad (Child 73) is banal enough: a triangular love-affair that ends in the death of all three lovers. It is the characters who hold the imagination – weak, fickle Lord Thomas, haughty, fair Eleanor, and the dark, vengeful bride with the dagger hidden in her wedding dress. During this century the ballad has quite frequently been found over an area bounded by Devon, Herts, Hereford, and Staffs. Also several Scottish sets are known. It is interesting that most of the English versions, and all the numerous American ones, obviously derive from a broadside text published during the reign of Charles II and often reprinted. Scholars incline to consider oral transmission to be almost a *sine qua non* of folk song diffusion, but ballads such as this remind us that word-of-mouth is far from being the only way in which folk songs have been traditionally passed on. In Scotland this ballad is sometimes called *Fair Annet*. It must be said that some of the Scottish oral versions hold beauties lacking in the texts under influence of print: such, for instance, as this embellishment to the description of Annet's grand journey to Lord Thomas's wedding:

> There were four and twenty gray goshawks
> A-flaffin their wings sae wide,
> To flaff the stour fra off the road
> That fair Annie did ride.

In the version of the text printed here, Mrs Pond's words have been expanded from versions collected by Hammond from Mrs Rowsell, of Taunton, Somerset, in 1905 (FSJ II 105), and by Sharp from Mrs Cockram, of Meshaw, Devon, in 1904 (FSJ II 107). Other versions have been found in oral tradition in Hampshire (FSJ II 106), Somerset (FSJ II 109), Hertfordshire (FSJ V 130–1), Staffordshire (SFL 651), and Gloucestershire (FSUT 135–7). Kidson (KTT 40) reports a Yorkshire version with words from a broadside of *c*. 1740.

Lovely Joan (FSJ IV 90)

Many of our amatory folk songs show a double sentiment of gaiety and irony that comes as a surprise to those expecting merely yokel quaintness. The young lady may show herself at a loss over the conduct of a false lover, but, confronted with importunity, she remains as a rule unruffled, completely mistress of herself. And if the subterfuges she adopts are of doubtful honesty, the implied judgement is that she is a smart girl and it serves that young fellow right. Thus, *Lovely Joan* seems to be sister to such resourceful girls as the heroine of the *Broomfield Hill* or of the traditional sets of *Blow Away the Morning Dew*. The song has been taken from oral tradition in Sussex (FSJ I 270), Suffolk (FSJ IV 330), Somerset (SFS IV 48), and Wiltshire (WUT 46). The text, hitherto published only in modified form, is completed here from the MS collection of Cecil Sharp.

Lucy Wan (JEFDSS I 53)

This rare ballad, also called *Lizzie Wan*, belongs to the same tradition as the well-known *Edward*. But whereas in *Edward* it is usually the brother who is the victim (for reasons that are seldom clear), in *Lizzie* or *Lucy Wan* it is the sister, guilty of incest whether wittingly or not, who is savagely put to death. This is the only version of the ballad found in oral tradition in England, nor has any new Scottish version been reported since the publication of Motherwell's *Minstrelsy* in 1827. The ballad is No. 51 in Child. The three opening stanzas are quoted from Child (with 'Lucy' substituted for 'Lizzie'), and the order of Mrs Dann's verses is re-arranged for the sake of coherence.

The Manchester 'Angel' (FSJ VII 52)

The Angel Inn is said to have stood in the Market Place adjoining Market Sted Lane, Manchester. According to Miss Anne Gilchrist, 'it seems possible that this song dates from about the '45. In November 1745 a Manchester regiment was raised in support of Charles Edward's cause, but suffered disaster with the Prince after the fiasco at Derby, surrendering at Carlisle a few weeks later.' Other versions of the song have been found in Dorset (FSJ VII 52–3) and in Yorkshire (KPS 4).

The Man of Burningham Town (FSJ IV 84)

Another homilectic ballad that, like *The Daughter of Peggy* and *On Monday Morning*, treats of a drastic cure for errant wives. Among H. E. D. Hammond's manuscripts is a version of this song (called *The Man of Dover*) collected in Dorset in 1905. E. J. Moeran published a Norfolk version (FSJ VII 8). Our words are filled out from these two sets. The singer sang 'Burningham', apparently meaning Burnham (on Crouch), not Birmingham.

The Mermaid (FSJ III 47)

The superstition that the sight of a mermaid is an omen of shipwreck is ancient and widespread, yet songs that treat of it are few. There is no sign that *The Mermaid* is older than the eighteenth century, but it has persisted in many forms, in both England and Scotland, in oral tradition, on broadsides, in song-books. It has been used as a sea-shanty, also as a students' song and a children's game ('The big ship sails up the Alley, Alley O'). Perhaps because of its familiarity in print, commentators and collectors have rather neglected this song, which, in good versions, has its fine points. The ballad is No. 289 in Child. It has been reported in recent years, from Oxfordshire (WUT 84), Hampshire (Gillington, *Old Hampshire Singing Games*), Cheshire (FSJ III 49), Dorset (FSJ III 50–1), Devonshire (FSJ III 139), and, in a common fragment, from Berkshire (FSJ V 227).

Mother, Mother, Make my Bed (FSJ V 135)

There has been argument whether this ballad derives from *Lady Maisry* or *Lord Lovel*. The manner of the lady's impending death, which would provide the essential clue, is missing. We do not know whether she is to be put to death on account of her disgrace (like Lady Maisry) or is pining for her lover's absence (like Lord Lovel's sweetheart). It hardly matters. In the version of Mrs Ford, a Sussex blacksmith's wife, the ballad is a good one. It has also been found in Somerset (FSJ I 44), Dorset (FSJ III 74–6), and Hants (FSJ III 304–6).

The New York Trader (FSJ VII 2)

Britain has a group of ballads in which a criminal on board a ship is detected by supernatural means. These include *Brown Robyn's Confession* (Child 57), *The Gosport Tragedy*, *Sir William Gower*, and *William Glenn*, with which the *New York Trader* is sometimes confused. In fact, all three latter songs seem to derive from an older ballad called *The Pirate*, in which the ship is bound for New Barbery, not for 'New York in Ameriky'. *The New York Trader* evidently enjoyed a vogue in the nineteenth century. It was frequently published by provincial broadside firms, and Catnach, in London, found it worth issuing at least three times. Alfred Williams collected a version in Wiltshire (WUT 265–6) and Cecil Sharp reported two Somerset versions of the closely related *Sir William Gower* (FSJ V 263–4). The ballad called *The Sailor and the Ghost* or *The Man and the Two Maidens* (FSJ VII 46–7) belongs to the same family of songs.

O Shepherd, O Shepherd (FSJ III 122)

From the form of this song, Miss Anne Gilchrist suspected that it may once have been a singing game – perhaps in the form of the advancing and retiring line – with one person playing the shepherd to whom inducements are offered to persuade him to return home. Various early Scottish compilers (Johnson, Herd, Chambers) printed versions of the song, though we have found no other English set than this. The tune is interesting as being a modal version of *Greensleeves*. Either the well-known version is a modal tune 'improved' by an ignorant musician, or else it has here been converted into a modal tune by a country singer.

The Old Man from Lee (JEFDSS III 130)

The old man's courtship is an ancient joke of which country folk never seemed to tire. In a form similar to the one we publish, the song appeared in the *Musical Miscellany* (London) in 1730. It seems to be widespread in Scotland, and Sharp found it common in the West Country. Versions have been reported from Yorkshire (KTT 92; FSJ II 273), Worcestershire (Folklore x 173–4), and Wiltshire (WUT 73). Our text is amplified from the Wiltshire version.

On Monday Morning (FSJ III 315)

Baring Gould, who describes this as a song 'relished by married men', found an early set in a collection of stall balladry, *West Country Garlands*, date about 1760. He obtained a version from the singing of Robert Hard of South Brent, Devon, which he called *A Week's Work Well Done* (BGSW 238–9). Our version is sung to a variant of the well-known *Turpin Hero* tune. Frank Kidson had information that the song was sung by Grimaldi the clown, about 1820.

One Night as I Lay on My Bed (FSJ III 78)

This piece belongs to a sizeable family of night-visit songs (called *Fensterlieder* – window songs – in Germany). It is related in theme to the well-known *Go from my Window, Go*, quoted in Beaumont and Fletcher's *Knight of the Burning Pestle* (1613), and before that, parodied as a sacred piece in *Ane Compendious Booke of Godly and Spirituall Songs* (1567). There, the scene is translated to Paradise. The importunate caller at the window is a sinner whom God first refuses but eventually admits by the door. Burns found a three-verse fragment, resembling part of our Dorset version, which he sent to Johnson for publication in *The Scots Musical Museum*, and, on the evidence of Allan Cunningham's *Works of Burns* (1834), the poet probably knew another version, from Nithsdale, ending with the familiar lovers' vow that the seas shall dry and the fishes fly and the rocks melt in the sun before one proves false to the other. Baring Gould prints a Devonshire version of *Go from my Window*, with the words re-written, under the title *Come to my Window*. Barrett has a version in BF described by Miss M. Dean-Smith as 'little altered since (it) appeared in the *Fitzwilliam Virginal Book*'. A Sussex fragment collected by W. P. Merrick is in FSJ I 269. The Somerset song *Arise Arise you Drowsy Maiden* in SFS IV is also related. From stanza 2 onward, our text is from Mr House of Beaminster, Dorset, collected by H. E. D. Hammond in 1906 (FSJ III 79–80).

The Outlandish Knight (FSJ IV 123)

This ballad has many titles. Scholars know it as *Lady Isabel and the Elf Knight* or *May Colvin*, but *An Outlandish Rover*, *The Highway Robber*, *The Old Beau*, are among titles preferred by folk singers. Child, who published it as No. 4 in his collection, noted it as one of the most widespread of ballads, with relatives in Poland, Germany, Scandinavia, France, the Netherlands (as *Halewijn*), and elsewhere, as far afield as Australia. It is also among the most persistent, being not infrequently sung today. Some scholars see in it traces of the Bluebeard story, others believe it may be an off-shoot of the legend of Judith and Holofernes. Perhaps more plausible is the theory that the ballad is descended from a folk-tale about a malevolent water-spirit who transforms himself into a knight and marries a girl with the intention of carrying her off to his watery home. The genial incident of the dialogue with the parrot (borrowed from Oriental tradition?) was isolated and made into a comic stage song, called *Tell-Tale Polly* (*c.* 1860). Within this century, besides our Norfolk set, versions have been printed from Westmorland (FSJ II 282), Yorkshire (three versions, FSJ II 282–3), Herefordshire (FSJ IV 122), Herts (FSJ IV 118), Sussex (FSJ IV 121), Wilts (WUT 159–61), and Somerset (four versions, FSJ IV 119–21; Sharp reported that he had found twenty-three sets of it in that county), Devon (FSJ IV 119), and Cornwall (FSJ IV 116–17). A fragmentary version in Manx is printed in FSJ VII 301.

T'Owd Yowe wi' one Horn (FSJ II 79)

The words of this song do not amount to much more than a mild piece of country humour. It may be a come-down version of a once-impressive piece, but if so, its former glory has faded out of sight. Yet the shape of the verse and the classical ballad ring of the tune indicate a noble ancestry. We print it mainly for the sake of the melody, which deserves wider recognition. At the same time, many will smile at the mutton-headed pugnacity of the indomitable 'owd yowe'. Percy Grainger recorded this at a folk-song competition in Brigg, Lincs. It won third prize. This seems to be the only version reported from oral tradition.

Oxford City (FSJ II 162)

Perhaps this song celebrated a real life tragedy. It often appeared on broadsides in the nineteenth century, published by Catnach and Such of London, Harkness of Preston, and Jackson of Birmingham. Other versions have been found in oral tradition in Essex (FSJ II 157), Sussex (FSJ II 200), and Dorset (FSJ VII 41), with two further texts from Somerset and

Dorset, collected by H. E. D. Hammond (FSJ VII 42–3). Our text is completed from these several versions.

The Ploughman (FSJ II 190)

This song started out, as some songs will, with intent to end otherwise. Mr Burstow's first verse was originally:

> It's of a pretty wench that came running 'long a trench,
> And sweetheart she could not get one,
> 'When there's many a dirty sow a sweetheart has got now,
> And I, a pretty wench, can't get one, get one, get one,
> And I, a pretty wench, can't get one.'

Here we are on familiar ground, for the beginning is that of the well-known *Condescending Lass*, often printed on broadsides, and not infrequently met with in the mouths of country singers to this day. *The Condescending Lass* belongs to the size-able family of songs on the theme of 'I wouldn't marry a . . .'. In it the girl reviews men of various trades, and rejects them all until she finds one whom she will deign to consider. But the present version loses sight of this theme, and from verse two onwards forgets all about the pernickety girl, settling down to a eulogy of the ploughman's trade, though here and there the words still recall those of *The Condescending Lass*. For the sake of coherence we have abandoned Mr Burstow's first verse and given it another title (he called it: *Pretty Wench*). A Wiltshire version of *The Condescending Lass* is given in WUT 122.

Ratcliffe Highway (FSJ II 172)

In the first half of the nineteenth century, Ratcliffe Highway, Stepney, was the toughest thoroughfare in the East End of

London. It was a place of sailors' lodging-houses, sailors' pubs, sailors' ladies. Henry Mayhew has given us vivid descriptions of the Highway, with tall brazen-faced women dressed in gaudy colours, sly pimps and crimps, roaring sailors out for a good time, bearded foreign musicians from the fifteen dance halls of the locality, and the intrepid policemen of H Division walking through the throng in twos. The *Ratcliffe Highway* song may have been made for performances in ships foc'sles, or it may have been made to impress the patrons of the Eastern Music Hall, the British Queen, the Prussian Eagle, or another local public house licensed for music. In any case, it now has some of the ring of tradition and much of the ring of truth. Mrs Howard's text is supplemented from an unpublished version collected in Sussex in 1954 and kindly communicated by R. Copper, and from a broadside by Catnach.

The Red Herring (FSJ V 284)

A nonsense song of the sort of *The Mallard, The Jolly Old Hawk, The Sow Took the Measles*, and *The Hunting of the Wren* (a well-known foreign relative is the French-Canadian *Alouette*). Perhaps at one time these pieces were by no means nonsensical, but accompanied a magic ritual connected with a sacred beast. The primitive dance tunes usually associated with this kind of song, remarked upon by Miss Lucy Broadwood, may point to a former ceremonial use. Whatever the case, to singers nowadays *The Red Herring* is merely a piece of amiable tomfoolery. Cecil Sharp printed three versions from Somerset (FSJ 20, 283–5) and a version from Wiltshire is in WUT 167.

Robin Hood and the Pedlar (FSJ II 156)

The text given here is very slightly amended from that collected by Lucy Broadwood from Mr Burstow of Horsham, Sussex. The song of Robin Hood's encounter with the battling pedlar was printed on broadsides by Such and Catnach in the nineteenth century, in much the same version as Mr Burstow sang it. In earlier forms of this ballad (as in Child 128) the outlaw's redoubtable antagonist is not a pedlar but a young gentleman dressed in silk, with stockings of shining scarlet, named Young Gamwell. 'Gamwell' and 'Gamble Gold' are thought to be corruptions of Gamelyn, and the story may be a come-down fragment of the manuscript *Tale of Gamelyn* (*c.* 1340). Other versions are printed from Essex (FSJ II 155) and Yorkshire (FSJ V 94).

Rounding the Horn (FSJ V 165)

Mr Bolton, an old sailing ship shantyman, had a remarkably fine repertory of sea-songs (see, for instance, pp. 44 and 48 of this collection). Somewhat to our surprise, we have not found any other published version of *Rounding the Horn*. The song seems to have been rather well known among nineteenth-century seamen. Miss Gilchrist collected another version in which the ship is called the *Conway*. In 1793, the crew of a ship called *Amphitrite* addressed a petition to the authorities complaining about the floggings ordered by the mate, 'a most Cruel and Barberous man'. The song may be a little later, though it is hard to be sure in these matters. The use of the description 'frigate' would imply that the vessel was a naval one. On the other hand, the reference may be to the brig *Amphitrite*, built in 1820 and engaged in the South American trade. The tune, a mixolydian come-all-ye melody, is a variant of *The Painful Plough*, and of the carol, *Come All You Worthy Christian Men*. It is also used for some sets of the convict transportation ballad, *Van Diemen's Land*.

The Royal Oak (FSJ V 167)

Baring Gould obtained a version of this song in the West Country. His singer called it *The Marigold*, and named the captain 'Sir Thomas Merrifield' of Bristol. In a broadside text quoted in Firth's *Naval Songs and Ballads* 87, and also in a version printed by Gavin Greig in his *Folk-Song of the North-East*, the ship is again the *Marigold*, and its master is given as 'Captain Mansfield of Bristol town'. Firth suggests that the reference may be to Captain Michael Mansfield, mentioned in Charnock's *Biographia Navalis* I 348, and that the action of the song is 'probably based on Kempthorne's repulse of the seven Algerine ships, December 29, 1669'. The name *Royal Oak* seems to have crept into the song by accident.

The Sailor from Dover (FSJ VIII 4)

Child has a ballad called *The Brown Girl* (295) which is like the *Dover Sailor* in reverse, for there it is the man who first scorns the girl, then falls sick with love for her, and the girl arrives and mocks his situation. There is some argument as to whether *The Dover Sailor* is sufficiently distinct to be reckoned as a separate song. The song has not often been reported since Child's time; apart from the present Somerset version, the only other printed set is in KG 20. Both versions seem to derive from the broadside *Sally and her True Love Billy* (issued without imprint). In America, where the song is more common, it is also called *A Brave Irish Lady*. The 'doctor' stanza seems to impress singers deeply; Sharp found an

Appalachian version in which the lover actually appears as a physician.

A Sailor in the North Country (FSJ II 194)

We have not found any other published set of this song, either in the British collections or those of the North Atlantic seaboard (though it is the kind of song that often found favour among the maritime communities of Newfoundland and Nova Scotia). It appeared not infrequently on nineteenth-century broadsides, though from its graces we presume it is of rather earlier composition. In her rendering of the opening phrase of the song, Mrs Verrall may have had in mind her version of the tune of *Salisbury Plain* (q.v.).

A Sailor's Life (FSJ I 99)

This favourite song has an obscure connexion with another popular piece sometimes called *Died for Love* (from which the students' song *There is a Tavern in the Town* has descended). Though it lacks the central story of the girl's ocean search for her sweetheart, *Died for Love* has a similar tune, and some versions use the opening stanza of *A Sailor's Life*. In revenge, some sets of *A Sailor's Life* borrow the conclusion of the other song, with the girl directing that her grave be dug wide and deep, and a white turtle dove be put on it, to show that she 'died for love'. In fact, various singers seem to have 'cross-pollenated' the two songs in several ways. Mr Hills's version has the story at once completer and more concisely than usual, and less contaminated with *Died for Love*. In England, the song has also been reported, sometimes under the titles of *Sweet William* or *Early, Early All in the Spring*, from Lincoln-shire (FSJ II 293–4), Dorset (FSJ VIII 212), Worcestershire (BCS

74–5), Somerset (SEF II), and Suffolk (MSS 26–9). Kidson (KG 92) prints a set of unidentified origin. Pitts and Catnach both published broadsides of the song (the latter called it *The Sailor Boy and his Faithful Mary*). It seems particularly common in the United States, and has been adapted to the life of timber-raftsmen.

Salisbury Plain (FSJ II 196)

The highwayman's 'goodnight' ballad, in which the hero turns robber to support his wife and ends up on the gallows, was a favourite with eighteenth- and nineteenth-century fairground singers and balladmongers. Such ballads were usually announced as 'the dying testament' of some well-known thief. The present song gains piquancy through being put in the mouth of the robber's sweetheart. The words as given here were obtained by Ralph Vaughan Williams from Mr Henry Burstow of Horsham, Sussex, a neighbour of Mr and Mrs Verrall, whose tune we include. Miss Lucy Broadwood had attempted to notate the song from Mr Burstow in 1893, but he had been too shy to sing her even one line of the words, and in consequence he had only been able to hum and whistle the tune confusedly. The experience, wrote Miss Broadwood, 'proves how impossible it is for country singers to detach tunes from words'. Variants of this melody have wandered all over Europe, seeming to have a common ancestor in the fifteenth-century Burgundian basse danse *Le petit roysin* (see W. Wiora, *Europäischer Volksgesang*, Cologne, 1952, p. 50). Five more Sussex versions are in FSJ II 197 and IV 323–4. Miss Broadwood's transcription of Mr Burstow's tune is in FSJ I 150. In the FSJ Index, the song is confused with another, quite distinct, piece called *The Blues*.

The Ship in Distress (FSJ IV 321)

The Portuguese ballad *A Nau Catarineta* and the French *La Courte Paille* tell much the same story. The ship has been long at sea, and food has given out. Lots are drawn to see who shall be eaten, and the captain is left with the shortest straw. The cabin boy offers to be sacrificed in his stead, but begs first to be allowed to keep look-out till the next day. In the nick of time he sees land (*'Je vois la tour de Babylone, Barbarie de l'autre côté'*) and the men are saved. Thackeray burlesqued this song in his *Little Billee*. It is likely that the French ballad gave rise to *The Ship in Distress*, which appeared on nineteenth-century broadsides. George Butterworth obtained four versions in Sussex (FSJ IV 320–2) and Sharp printed one from James Bishop of Priddy, Somerset (SFS III 64), with 'in many respects the grandest air' which he had found in that county. The text comes partly from Mr Bishop's version, and partly from a broadside.

Six Dukes Went a-Fishing (FSJ III 170)

To folk-singers, the drowned man in this song is either the Duke of Grantham, or Grafton, or Bedford. Miss Lucy Broadwood suggests (FSJ III 176–9) that he may have been in fact William de la Pole, first Duke of Suffolk who in 1450 was murdered by his political enemies, and his body flung upon the sea-shore at Dover. (Shakespeare writes his version in *Henry VI, Part II*, Act 4.) The 'black was their mourning' stanza occurs also in the ballad of *The Death of Queen Jane*, presumably being borrowed from *Six Dukes* if, as seems probable, the latter is the older song. Other 'borrowings' from this ballad appear in a broadside of 1690, called *The Noble Funeral of the Renowned Champion the Duke of Grafton who was Slain at the*

Siege of Cork and *Royally Interred in Westminster Abbey. To the Tune of, Fond Boy: or, Loves a Sweet Passion. (Printed for Charles Bates at the Sun and Bible in Py-Corner.)* Grainger recorded three versions in Lincolnshire (FSJ III 170–4) and Sharp found one (of Yorkshire origin) in the Marylebone Workhouse, London (FSJ V 79).

The Streams of Lovely Nancy (FSJ VII 59)

Our text has been amended and filled out with fragments from various sources, notably from Sussex versions obtained by Miss A. G. Gilchrist, and Francis Jekyll and George Butterworth (FSJ IV 310–11). Even so its meaning is far from clear. W. P. Merrick also reported the song from Sussex (FSJ I 122) as did Lucy Broadwood (BCS 136, under the title *Faithful Emma*). Baring Gould prints a West Country set in BGSW as *The Streams of Nantsian*. All these, and the broadsides by Catnach, Pitt, and Such, are equally incoherent and mysterious. Miss Broadwood suggests that the song originated in Cornwall, and that the 'little streamers that walk the meadows gay' may be young tin-miners, boys or girls, who 'stream' or wash the ore. Both she and Miss Gilchrist (in FSJ IV 312–19) detect traces of an old mystical original in this curious song. Certain details of its setting are reminiscent of 'The Castle of Love and Grace', a parabolic representation of the Virgin, in the fourteenth-century poem, *Cursor Mundi*. Miss Gilchrist offers persuasive evidence that 'in the *Streamers* we might have an unrecognized relic of a hymn to Mary'.

The Trees they Grow So High (FSJ II 95)

This is one of the most curious, most beautiful, and most widespread of British ballads. Some fifty years ago, Kidson reported it as 'common all over the country', and it is not infrequently met with nowadays, especially in Scotland and Ireland. Sharp alone collected a dozen sets of it. Perhaps the fullest printed texts are Scottish, though English and Irish sets include stanzas not found in Scottish versions. It is sometimes said that the ballad is based on the actual marriage of the juvenile laird of Craigton to a girl several years his senior, the laird dying three years later in 1634. But in fact the ballad may be older; indeed, there is no clear evidence that it is Scottish in origin. Child marriages for the consolidation of family fortunes were not unusual in the Middle Ages and in some parts the custom persisted far into the seventeenth century. The presenting and wearing of coloured ribbons, once common in Britain, still plays a prominent part in betrothal and marriage in Central and Eastern Europe. For some reason this ballad, so common in Britain, is very rare in the U.S.A. The melody given is in the Phrygian mode, seldom met with in English folk song (a different tune to these words, in BGSW 8–9 is also Phrygian). Only one stanza of Miss Bidder's version has survived. The greater part of the text we print comes from the versions sung to Sharp by Harry Richards of Curry Rivell, Somerset, in 1904 (FSJ II 44–6), and to Lucy Broadwood by Mrs Joiner, of Chiswell Green, Herts, in 1914 (FSJ V 190). In FSJ, further versions will be found from Surrey (I 14–15), Somerset (II 46–7), Sussex (II 206), Yorkshire (II 274), and Dorset (II 275).

The Whale-Catchers (FSJ I 101)

This song is sometimes confused with the one called *The Greenland Whale Fishery*, though in fact the two pieces are separate. From its reference to London, it would seem that *The Whale-Catchers* may once have belonged to the whalemen who sailed out of the Greenland Dock, in Deptford. The version follows the usual pattern of whaling songs – the departure, hard times on the whaling grounds, the rowdy return to port – but it lacks the graphic detail of the chase that distinguishes *The Greenland Whale Fishery*. 'Imez' is written as the singer pronounced it, but we have not traced the where-abouts of this place. This seems to be the only version of the song recovered from oral tradition.

When I was a Little Boy (JEFDSS VI I)

Though this topsy turvy song was collected in the Shetlands, it seems to be English enough to qualify for inclusion here. The suggestion has been made that it is a folk song converted into a comic song for the amusement of London audiences. It belongs to the great family of 'Songs of Marvels' or 'Songs of Lies', along with *The Derby Ram, A Shoulder of Mutton Jumped over from France* (FSJ V 292) and, in America, *Nottamun Town*. The present song is found in America, entitled *The Little Brown Dog*.

When I Was Young (JEFDSS IV 5)

The widespread song about the joyful maid who becomes a sorrowful wife would seem to be quite old (in some versions she wears shoes of 'spanish black' and a girdle that sold for a hundred pounds). Possibly its persistence was helped by its inclusion in a popular songster, *Sam Cowell's 120 Comic Songs*, about 1850. The even wider-known song from the man's point of view, *When I was Single, Oh Then*, presumably sprang from this. Besides this Durham version, sets have been reported from North Yorkshire (KTT 156), Devonshire (JEFDSS III 51), and 'the West Country' (*Word Lore* Vol. 2, 1927). A version of the male counterblast from Oxfordshire is in WUT III.

Ye Mar'ners All (FSJ III 116)

The raffish words of this song were in print in 1838 or shortly after, in one of a set of miniature penny song-books called *Little Warblers*, published by Ryle of Seven Dials, London. The handsome melody is a variant of a tune used for the well-known *Died for Love*. Barratt prints a Wiltshire version called *A Jug of This* in BF. Hammond at first understood Mrs Russell to sing 'Ye *mourners* all' but later presumed that she meant 'mariners'. Mrs Russell's words were fragmentary, and Hammond filled out the text from a version supplied by W. Haines 'of Halfway House between Sherborne and Yeovil'.

The Young and Single Sailor (FSJ IV 128)

This is an (eighteenth-century?) adaptation of the old half-ring story, widespread in European balladry. It was published on various broadsides, notably by Such, and appears in *The Vocal Library* songbook published in London in 1822. The well-known *Fair Phoebe and her Dark Eyed Sailor*, probably a stage song of the 1830s, derives from this ballad, which is also reported from oral tradition in Hampshire (FSJ IV 127), Herefordshire (FSJ IV 128), Dorset and Sussex (FSJ IV 129), and Somerset (SFS II 40). FSJ VI 272 offers an Irish version.

Young Edwin in the Lowlands Low (FSJ III 266)

This ballad was evidently a great favourite, for versions of it were printed on balladsheets by many printers in England, Scotland, and Ireland. Several versions have been found in the North-east and the upland South of America. The hero is variously given as Young Edwin, Young Edward, and Young

Edmund. Mrs Hopkins's tune is sometimes used for the carol
Come, all you worthy Christians (e.g. FSJ I 74). It appears to be
related to the well-known *Dives and Lazarus* melody (perhaps
both are descended from a common ancestor). Other English
versions have been reported from oral tradition in Sussex (FSJ
I 124) and Hampshire (GFH 38). A Canadian set collected by
Maud Karpeles is given in FSJ VIII 227–8.

The Young Girl Cut Down in her Prime (FSJ IV 325)

At the end of the eighteenth century a homilectic street ballad
spread in England concerning the death and ceremonial
funeral of a soldier 'disordered' by a woman. It was called
The Unfortunate Rake (in Ireland) or *The Unfortunate Lad* (on
the broadside printed by Such). Many singers know it as
St James's Hospital. It is still a common song in the British
Army, though printed versions are few English sets have been
reported from Yorkshire (FSJ I 254) and Hampshire (FSJ III
292). Our song represents a later development, in which the
sexes are reversed, but the ceremonial funeral is retained.
Versions of this form have been recorded from Oxfordshire
and Somerset (FSJ IV 326) as well as the present Hampshire
version. In America, the song has been adapted to the cattle
range (*The Cowboy's Lament* or *The Streets of Laredo*) and
the gambling hall (*St James' Infirmary*). The motive of the
ceremonial funeral remains constant, despite all the trans-
formations of the chief character.

Many of the songs in this book are included
in the 12″ L.P. recorded by A. L. Lloyd on
Collector label JGB 5001.

Bibliography

Books to Read

Fox-Strangways, A. H., and Karpeles, Maud. *Cecil Sharp* (2nd ed.). London (O.U.P.), 1955.

Lloyd, A. L. *The Singing Englishman: an introduction to folk-song*. London (Workers' Music Association), n.d.

Nettel, Reginald. *Sing a Song of England: a social history of traditional song*. London (Phoenix House), 1954.

Reeves, James. *The Idiom of the People*. English traditional verse from the manuscripts of Cecil J. Sharp. London (Heinemann), 1958.

Sharp, Cecil James. *English Folk Song: some conclusions* (3rd ed.). London (Methuen), 1954.

Wells, Evelyn K. *The Ballad Tree: a study of British and American ballads, their folklore, verse, and music*. London (Methuen), 1950.

Also relevant, particularly for the chapter on 'Our Songs and their Folklore':

Alford, Violet. *Introduction to English Folklore*. London (Bell), 1952.

Books to Refer to

Bronson, Bertrand H. *The Traditional Tunes of the Child Ballads*, Vol. 1. Princeton, N. J. (University Press), 1959.

Chappell, William. *Popular Music of the Olden Time* (2 vols.). n.d. (1858–9).

CHILD, Francis James. *English and Scottish Popular Ballads* (reprinted in three vols.). New York (Folklore Press), 1957.

DEAN-SMITH, Margaret. *A Guide to English Folk Song Collections, 1822–1952, with an index to their contents, historical annotations, and an introduction.* Liverpool (University Press), 1954.

Journal of the English Folk Dance and Song Society (1932, in progress).

Journal of the Folk Song Society (1899–1931).

Folk Song Collections Containing Useful Notes or Other Information

BARING GOULD, S., and others. *A Garland of Country Song.* London (Methuen), 1895.

BARING GOULD, S., and others. *Songs of the West* (revised ed.). London (Methuen), 1905.

BROADWOOD, Lucy E. *English County Songs.* London (Cramer), 1893.

BROADWOOD, Lucy E. *English Traditional Songs and Carols.* London (Boosey), 1908.

BRUCE, J. Collingwood, and STOKOE, J. *Northumbrian Minstrelsy.* Newcastle upon Tyne (Society of Antiquaries), 1882.

KIDSON, Frank. *Traditional Tunes.* Oxford (Taphouse), 1891.

LLOYD, A. L. *Come All Ye Bold Miners: ballads and songs of the coalfields.* London (Lawrence & Wishart), 1952.

SHARP, Cecil James. *English Folk Songs* (selected edn, 2 vols.). London (Novello), 1916.

SHARP, Cecil James. *Folk Songs from Somerset* (5 series). London (Simpkin Marshall and Barnicott & Pearce), 1905–19.

WILLIAMS, Alfred. *Folk Songs of the Upper Thames.* London (Duckworth), 1923. *This collection contains texts only.*

Index of First Lines

THE STORY OF PENGUIN CLASSICS

Before 1946 ...'Classics' are mainly the domain of academics and students, without readable editions for everyone else. This all changes when a little-known classicist, E. V. Rieu, presents Penguin founder Allen Lane with the translation of Homer's Odyssey that he has been working on and reading to his wife Nelly in his spare time.

1946 The Odyssey becomes the first Penguin Classic published, and promptly sells three million copies. Suddenly, classic books are no longer for the privileged few.

1950s Rieu, now series editor, turns to professional writers for the best modern, readable translations, including Dorothy L. Sayers's *Inferno* and Robert Graves's *The Twelve Caesars*, which revives the salacious original.

1960s 1961 sees the arrival of the Penguin Modern Classics, showcasing the best twentieth-century writers from around the world. Rieu retires in 1964, hailing the Penguin Classics list as 'the greatest educative force of the 20th century'.

1970s A new generation of translators arrives to swell the Penguin Classics ranks, and the list grows to encompass more philosophy, religion, science, history and politics.

1980s The Penguin American Library joins the Classics stable, with titles such as *The Last of the Mohicans* safeguarded. Penguin Classics now offers the most comprehensive library of world literature available.

1990s Penguin Popular Classics are launched, offering readers budget editions of the greatest works of literature. Penguin Audiobooks brings the classics to a listening audience for the first time, and in 1999 the launch of the Penguin Classics website takes them online to an ever larger global readership.

The 21st Century Penguin Classics are rejacketed for the first time in nearly twenty years. This world famous series now consists of more than 1,300 titles, making the widest range of the best books ever written available to millions – and constantly redefining the meaning of what makes a 'classic'.

The Odyssey continues ...

The best books ever written

PENGUIN 🐧 CLASSICS

SINCE 1946

Find out more at www.penguinclassics.com